WARREN JOHNSON
Chairman of the Geograp... ....g..... ....
University. He has published a number of articles on the
themes developed in this book in periodicals such as *Technol-
ogy Review, Equilibrium, Environmental Affairs, Sierra Club
Bulletin,* and in the book *Toward the Steady State Economy.*
He is the co-editor of *Economic Growth vs. The Environment.*

"A remarkably prescient work, one that sheds much needed
light on the economic transformation that lies ahead."

Lester R. Brown
Worldwatch Institute

"We are approaching a period of resource scarcity, but as
Warren Johnson lucidly illustrates, this does not mean the
end of the world. He believes in the resiliency of human
beings and sees, in the need to adapt to more frugal ways, the
opportunity for new lifestyles that will be happier because
they are richer in personal experiences. *Muddling Toward
Frugality* is loaded with information, yet pleasantly readable;
realistic about the forthcoming crises, yet reasonably hopeful."

René Dubos

"I welcome this book. Johnson makes a useful contribution
to the growing debate over the limits of economic growth."

Hazel Henderson, author of
Creating Alternative Futures

Muddling Toward Frugality

Warren Johnson

SHAMBHALA
BOULDER 1979

SHAMBHALA PUBLICATIONS, INC.
1123 Spruce Street
Boulder, Colorado 80302

Copyright © 1978 by Warren A. Johnson
Distributed in the United States by Random House
and in Canada by Random House of Canada Ltd.

LIBRARY OF CONGRESS CATALOGING IN PUBLICATION DATA
Johnson, Warren A.
Muddling toward frugality.
Reprint of the ed. published by Sierra Club Books,
San Francisco.
Includes bibliographical references and index.
I. Economic development. 2. Stagnation (Economics)
3. Human ecology. I. Title.
[HD82.J5943 1979]   330.1   79-5172
ISBN 0-87773-169-1
ISBN 0-394-73835-7 (Random House)

Printed in the United States of America

For Martha, Aaron, and Blake

Table of Contents

Preface: Heading Home 9

Chapter I
Neither Utopia Nor Oblivion 11

The Benefits of Barriers 14. The Inevitability of Adaptation 19
Muddling as Political Adaptation 23.

Chapter II
An Ecological View of History 29

Our Genetic Heritage: Hunters and Gatherers 32. The Fall from
the Garden: Agriculture 39. Making Agriculture Fit: The Elabora-
tion of Culture 44. Renewed Disequilibrium: The Modern Era 49.
The Prospects Ahead 53.

Chapter III
Advancing Technology, Declining Resources 55

The "Easy" Times 56. The Pleasures and Pitfalls of Abundance
61. Outlook on Resources: Minerals, Agriculture, and Energy 69.
Failing Technologies 90. Winning Technologies 97.

Chapter IV
The Subsidence 101

The Relative Price of Raw Materials and Labor 108. The Urban
Impact 113. Why Personal incomes Will Fall 116. The Question
of Employment 122. Adam Smith or Thomas Jefferson? 128.

Chapter V
The Theory and Practice of Muddling 137

Muddling Toward the Public Interest 139. The Benefits of Muddling 149.

Chapter VI
The Hazards of Muddling Toward Frugality 153

The Imagined Hazards of Muddling Through 154. The Real Hazards of Muddling Through 158.

Chapter VII
The Pace of Change 171

The Social Costs of Rapid Change 172. Frugality with a Vengeance 176. Easing into Frugality: A Guide to Urbanites 181. Plunging into Frugality: Problems of Pioneering 187. The Politics of Decentralization 196. The Need for Patience 200.

Chapter VIII
The Pros and Cons of Underdevelopment 203

How Population Growth in the Underdeveloped Countries Will End 211. Some Assets of Underdeveloped Countries 216. Two Questionable Gifts: Trade and Education 219. The End of Cultural Imperialism 227.

Chapter IX
Out of the Corner 229

The Futility of Resistance 230. Things Fall Together 235.

Acknowledgments 239
Reference Notes 241
Index 247

Heading Home

If we are to enjoy this planet for a long time, we may as well face the fact that trying to perpetuate the affluent society is going to be an uphill struggle. To maintain the heavy flow of raw materials now being cranked through our economy will become an increasingly laborious and ultimately desperate task. Affluence will grow less comfortable, and there will be less peace and security in it. If the earth is to be a true home for us, a place of refuge and nurture, we may as well start to think about how we can make it such a place. The task will not be as difficult as it may sound, and requires no wishful thinking about technological breakthroughs, effective government, or heightened human consciousness. We can move toward a secure, sustainable way of life easily if we accept the logic of frugality.

CHAPTER I

Neither Utopia Nor Oblivion

A growing element of fear haunts our thinking about the future of industrial society. With the emergence of chronic unemployment, rising prices, and unresolved social problems, some key factors affecting the basic conditions of our lives seem to be slipping beyond our control. The old utopian visions no longer move us, and new ones seem powerless before the momentum of modern industrial society. For the most part, we simply cling to the present rather than face the fearful prospect of deterioration and collapse.

This apprehensiveness is unfortunate since the future is not likely to be anywhere near as bleak as we tend to picture it; collapse is no more likely than utopia. These extremes are both contrary to human behavior. The same will-to-survive that works to prevent collapse and oblivion also works to thwart the utopian designs of a philosopher king. Life at all levels is a hurly-burly affair of getting on as well as possible in the circumstances living things find themselves in. Between the two extremes of utopia and oblivion is the whole of life. It is a wide area with many paths leading to different places. In today's world, some of these paths have the appearance of traditional cultures, while others are new. But all reflect the need to be frugal in the use of land and resources.

The origins of the word frugality in Latin are *frugalior,* meaning useful or worthy, and *frux,* meaning fruitful or productive. These meanings give the word a nice feeling, but unfortunately, the word has changed over the years, and has come to mean thriftiness, the abstention from luxury and lavishness. In this book, the word will be used in its original meaning — to suggest economic conditions in which society is obliged by the force of circumstances to make full and "fruitful" use of all its resources.

We are already being forced slowly and against our will to husband resources. Scarcity is the mechanism that is inexorably diverting industrial society from the path of sustained growth that has characterized the modern era. This scarcity will be reflected primarily in higher prices, and it will increasingly interfere with what we presently see as the orderly process of things. Our economy, our institutions, and our social values will all become less useful and will gradually be replaced by new ways that reflect the need to husband resources. Human skills and muscles will begin to replace fossil fuels. Small-scale, labor-intensive production will be increasingly competitive with the large, centralized, manufacturing operations that evolved under conditions of cheap energy and transportation.

People will slowly redistribute themselves to be able to utilize available land and resources more easily, and to avoid increasingly expensive transportation. As mobility is reduced, the traditional basis for responsibility to one's community and environment will be reestablished; people will have to live with the consequences of their actions rather than escape the effects by moving away. As communities become more necessary, the values that support them will strengthen, filling the void left by our growing disillusionment with modern values and the large-scale industrial economy. The timeless virtues of loyalty, cooperation, and selflessness — all thinly observed now — will once again be functional, as will the simple pleasures of family and friends, the knowledge of a trade, and the comforts of a well-known environment.

The future will perhaps be less spectacular than the optimists and the technologists may like to see it. They might speak of the loss of will to challenge obstacles, challenges our forebears would have relished, and they might lament the loss of the robust Renaissance spirit that was the mark of modern man and took Western civilization so far. But they might also forget that Machiavelli was as much a Renaissance figure as was da Vinci. By the same token, the future will be less dark and foreboding, less strange and alien than the pessimists see it. The fear of modern society collapsing from its own weight and rigidity will be reduced as the future evolves away from its present dependence on machines and toward a way of life that is down-to-earth and familiar; a life based on simplicity and the frugal use of resources. How good a life it will be depends largely on the quality of our adaptation to the barriers ahead of us.

The Benefits of Barriers

For my own part, I feel much better about the prospects for the future than I did a few years ago. At that time I held views that were much more on the dark side:

It is hard to escape the conclusion that the continuation of present patterns of economic growth will take us toward greater ecological instability and, sooner or later, into a period of chaos followed by the establishment of a balance at some lower level of population and productivity.[1]

The mistake, I now see, in this way of thinking was to assume that there was a difference, even a separation, between economics and ecology, and that the economy could go where it pleased uninhibited by ecological constraints until the whole economic order broke down. But the last few years have made it clear that the economy is heavily influenced by ecological factors, especially by the onset of scarcity. The evening news now gives close coverage to topics hardly mentioned a few years ago, such as the weather in agricultural regions, natural gas supplies, and the wholesale price index. The meetings of OPEC oil producers alone determine how many billions of dollars will flow out of the country. The economy does not function independent of ecological relationships, and we are not dependent on ecologists to tell us so; we all feel the pressures firsthand.

At times the workings of this "environmental resistance" — the resistance of the environment to additional growth — are hard to see because of our power to modify the environment and to create useful new resources. Political and economic questions also tend to get mixed up in resource issues, often dominating them. But even if the environmental mechanisms that restrain growth are not as directly expressed or as clear to us as they are in nature, they will make themselves felt.

This matter of environmental resistance deserves attention, for it is fundamental to our prospects for the future, to the confidence we will need to face the changes that will come. At all costs I wish to avoid wishful thinking on this matter. It is only by looking squarely at the forces at work in the world, both social and environmental, that anything will be gained to help us see where we are.

Ecology and economics have several characteristics in common. One of these is the necessity of dealing with the concept of general equilibrium (a concept whose meaning will become clearer as we proceed) to explain the world we live in. In a stimulating article comparing the similarities between economics and ecology, Kenneth Boulding describes general equilibrium as being like an elaborate computer program for

solving a vast number of equations.[2] In nature, the
equations govern birth and death rates of populations
in an ecosystem. In the economy, the analogous equations deal with products that are bought and sold.
Equilibrium occurs in either case when a solution is
found to all the equations; until then, the variables
must continue to change.

Once an equilibrium is reached, it may be very
stable. For example, when fish are removed from a
lake or trees harvested from a forest, the original equilibrium will usually reestablish itself after a period of
time. Or when resources managers try to change a site
from brush to grass, for instance, they often find it
difficult to sustain the change without continuous
effort as the original equilibrium, the brush, tends to
reestablish itself. The same tendencies hold for societies. During the Great Depression, the economy
seemed unresponsive to the efforts made to revive it.
Traditional or peasant societies often are resistant to
change; the products of long evolutions, their equilibrium sometimes frustrates planners who try to encourage development.

The difficulty of breaking out of a state of equilibrium is something that constrains most living things. But
from another point of view, this difficulty is com-
forting because it demonstrates the resilience of all
forms of life. The ability of insects to survive massive
doses of deadly chemicals, or of plants to recolonize
areas devastated by everything from volcanoes to nuclear explosions, and the ability of wild animals to

survive in suburbs — all should make us feel more confident about the resilience of nature. In the same way, human societies have survived natural disasters and devastating wars, often without major long-range effects, no matter how destructive they seemed at first.

Yet change does occur. Equilibriums are broken. How?

If a well-established equilibrium exists, the stimulus for change must come either from an outside source or from a mutation within the ecosystem that has developmental potential. Let us say that a new species of animal migrates into a natural environment and finds a niche that it can successfully occupy, possibly at the expense of other species. Its numbers grow rapidly as it colonizes the niche. These are the good times because the niche is open, food is available, and predators have not had time to respond. If we want to be anthropomorphic about it, we could say that this is the time when the new arrivals are fat and sassy. Perhaps they even ascribe some special qualities to their kind for their ability to do so well relative to other species in the environment. At this point, the system is not in equilibrium — the "computer" has not been able to come up with a solution to the data it has been given. Change continues; it cannot stop at this point which is ideal for the new arrivals. Slowly, things close in on them as the niche begins to fill up; food becomes scarce, predators arrive on the scene, and other pressures are felt. This is environmental resistance, and nothing can be done to escape it. While previously everything worked out well for the newcomers, at this stage nothing works out well; nothing can restore the good old days. Not only are there constraints on population growth, but the population may even be reduced, especially if the niche has been overexploited. Predators now find it easier to take the weak individuals, leaving only the strongest and most fit. In a sense, the population becomes dependent on predators to maintain it in good health and at a level within the carrying capacity of the environment.

An analogy with the modern era can be drawn. Starting with the Renaissance, modern man has expanded into a vast, unutilized niche made accessible by advances in science and technology. Part of the initial expansion was based on the military power that enabled Europeans to colonize much of the world, but much more stemmed from quantum increases in the knowledge of how to manipulate the environment in order to support larger populations. Our accomplishments have been staggering — there is no question of that — and perhaps the egoism and self-satisfaction that characterize our age are justified. But such pride cannot help against the impersonal forces of environmental resistance that are now appearing. We have passed the ideal point; our niche is filling up.

If the analogy with natural phenomena were fully applicable, there would be little concern over the future. Environmental resistance would slow economic and population growth until some carrying capacity established by the environment was reached. But our situation is unique. We are not only *filling* our niche, but we are *consuming* it as well by using up fossil fuels and other nonrenewable resources. Technology provides a credit to balance this loss to the degree that it can create resources out of formerly useless stuff and can thus expand the niche. But this is a process that is slowing today. One thing is certain; we will run into environmental resistance of some form or another, sooner or later. The question is: How will this resistance operate, and when will we feel its full impact?

Let us hope that the environmental resistance we run into will be the resistance of dwindling resources. The alternatives are worse — overpopulation, the buildup of poisons in the environment, the increasing scale of technology with all its totalitarian implications, social degeneration. We *need* the restraint provided by resource limitations. As with the dependency of many animals on their predators, we now approach the remarkable situation where the future well-being of humanity is dependent on the restraint and balance provided by the depletion of nonrenewable resources. There are no scapegoats; it is just the way things have worked out.

The Inevitability of Adaptation

Adaptation is necessary for the historical continuity of all living things. While it is true that organisms living in a stable, mature, natural environment may not need to adapt to survive, just as human beings in a stable cultural situation do not have to change very much, this certainly is not the situation we find ourselves in now. In a number of ways, the present world is far from a state of equilibrium. More than any single factor, the quality of the future will depend on the effectiveness of our adaptation to the forces of change that are at work in our world today — the wisdom and creativity that we put into finding a new balance.

Unlike the members of a traditional society, Americans are a relatively adaptable people. We have had to adapt steadily to the requirements of industrialism, and even though it has not always been a smooth adaptation, it does prove our flexibility. At times one could even get the impression that we are addicted to change, but this is belied by our intense resistance to basic political and economic shifts. It is safe to say that no society looks forward to fundamental change; it is just too threatening.

Luckily, adaptation is not an all-at-once, no-second-chance process. It is an ongoing process that entails a great many experiments, dead ends, and setbacks. It is far more a matter of muddling along than anything resembling planned social change. Evolution exhibits the same hit-or-miss characteristics. Superficially, it may appear inefficient as species evolve and then disappear. But in the long run, it is very efficient as species are replaced by others that are more successful in utilizing the opportunities the environment offers. In human terms, a better adaptation to existing conditions will make irrelevant much that has gone before, in the way that modern technology made obsolete many mining, logging, and farming communities. There was nothing that the people caught in these places could do. They could only encourage their young people to leave and to seek jobs elsewhere. The future may do the same thing to many of us and to many of the first efforts to adapt to frugality. But if time is available to permit these processes to proceed slowly, the necessity to adapt should not put an intolerable burden on any single generation. And technology should be able to play a very helpful role here, offsetting many scarcities as they appear and developing ways to utilize renewable resources.

Time is essential; the process of adaptation cannot be hurried. There is no substitute for time to try things out. There have been many ideas in the recent past that seemed so good at first but have not worked out: urban renewal, Operation Headstart, and pollution taxes are a few examples. Experience is a good teacher, but often a slow one. At other times, ideas that at first seemed to be insignificant ended up having tremendous impact. I think of Thoreau's essay on civil disobedience, which gave Gandhi a strategy for gaining independence for India. The same strategy was later utilized by the civil rights movement in the United States during the 1960s. It was an idea whose time had come, but it took many years to realize this, and there was no way of anticipating that it would happen.

What ideas will play the same role as we muddle toward frugality? Only time can supply the answer. If we go with the grain of the times and accept the limits of resources and environment, it seems safe to say that a number of generations should have time to explore different paths into the future and to develop methods of livelihood increasingly based on renewable resources, the only safe basis for a long human era. But if we resist change and try to deny the existence of scarcity in our push for continued growth, our remaining resources will be rapidly depleted and the necessary adaptation delayed, forcing a precipitous and dangerous rate of change later, something that may not be possible to accomplish without violence.

What are the human qualities that could lead to violence? Surprisingly, they are some of the qualities that have been most honored in Western civilization ever since the Renaissance. In a remarkable book titled *The Comedy of Survival,* Joseph Meeker distinguishes between two types of heroes, the tragic hero and the comic hero.[3] He describes them as they are depicted in classical literature, although we need not be restricted to this one source; it is a universal distinction. The tragic hero is the one we have tended to honor; the one who is willing to risk everything for a goal he knows to be right, who is unswerving in defense of moral principle, and who is not hesitant to take on powers greater than himself. Yet different people see the same situation differently, and such single-minded zeal has led to wars in the past. Today, terrorists who employ indiscriminate violence see themselves as risking their lives for a noble objective. It is this same mentality that is apt to challenge resource limits, rather than accept them. On top of all this, the tragic hero is usually an unpleasant individual to be with; he takes himself very seriously; he is unwilling to compromise; and he is condescending to anyone who disagrees with him.

In contrast, the comic hero is usually relegated to the status of a buffoon — base and silly, although innocuous. His goal is simply to survive and to enjoy himself as best he can. He is unwilling to fight; instead, he tries to outwit his enemies and the authorities. His victories are small; survival and life are what are important to him; no cause could be worth dying for. The comic hero is friendly toward life and takes things as they are; life is an end in itself, rather than a struggle between right and wrong. Meeker suggests that perhaps it is time that we honor these virtues. He argues that it is the comic hero who will better insure our survival — the human animal adapting to the world as it is and enjoying what it has to offer, rather than trying to make it over into something that it is not and cannot be. It has been said that true heroism is to see the world as it is and to love it. This would seem to be a valuable quality, and it may turn out to be the key to the successful adaptation to scarcity.

Muddling as Political Adaptation

It may seem ironic to look on the stumblings of government as an asset in coming to terms with the future, but given the general resistance to change in any society, an inefficient government actually protects us from the dangers inherent in sustained economic growth to the point of overgrowth. Governmental inefficiency encourages — even forces — individuals to take their lives into their own hands, or in other words, to adapt.

There is little question that if the government could plan effectively, it would plan for the preservation of the world as it is now — and for continued growth. After all, in this relatively free democratic society, growth benefits virtually everyone; it produces jobs, incomes, tax revenues for government, profits for business, and it reduces the burdens of welfare. The memory of the Great Depression is a powerful part of the broad political consensus that the most important job of government is to get the economy going and to put people back to work. Presidents are reelected or defeated on the basis of their handling of the economy. Conservation issues are decided by their impact on the economy. Those measures that put people to work — on dams, pollution-control programs, improving parks — find much better acceptance than programs that threaten to slow the economy by restricting the use of resources, or by closing industrial plants that degrade the environment. If economic planning were more effective, economic growth would be faster and steadier, thereby increasing the danger of overgrowth now and precipitous changes later.

Fortunately, this kind of governmental effectiveness is not likely. Not only is our ability to plan limited, but natural tendencies are on the side of economic slow-down and forced adaptation to scarcities. It is not possible to deny the reality of declining oil and gas production, high prices for imported materials, and the huge capital costs to develop new energy sources. When we try to deny this reality, as we do when we place price controls on oil and natural gas, we only cause consumption to go up and create a greater imbalance with existing energy supplies.

Politicians are caught in a predicament; they are asked to keep prices down, to conserve energy, and to get the economy going. But it is not possible to do all of these things at once, and responsible political decisions are likely to be unpopular. Such dilemmas reflect, more than anything else, the contradictions of a growth-oriented economy operating under conditions of raw material scarcity.

Politicians are likely to find their difficulties getting worse as time passes and scarcity presses harder on us. They will have to deal with the thankless task of dividing up a pie that is becoming smaller; they will have to make cuts in existing programs, probably without reducing taxes, even as prices are increasing. Available funds will more and more be absorbed by programs no one ever expected would take so much of the federal budget: programs to develop new energy sources, to prop up faltering employment, and to deal with skyrocketing welfare and unemployment costs. A number of politicians, unable to satisfy their supporters, will find themselves out of a job.

Realistic planning that accepts the constraints of limited resources will be unpopular and resisted. Who will want to plan for stability or, worse yet, decline, especially after this period of our greatest power and influence? But when the struggle to prop up a way of life that is no longer practical becomes too great, a new economic orientation will emerge. It will receive the same reluctant commitment that Americans finally gave to the withdrawal from Vietnam; it will be preferable to more adverse economic and political reactions that threaten to tear the country apart. Contrary to the lament of frustrated promoters of change, politicians will act, but not until the writing is so clearly on the wall that they and, more important, their constituents cannot miss it. Once this realization is reached, the world will be seen in a new way. At that point, we will be over the hump, and the political decisions that follow can be expected to be more of a help than a hindrance.

In the meantime, the inability of government to resolve the problems facing us will encourage individuals to think about ways to secure a safe niche for themselves, rather than relying on government to take care of them. It is the prudent thing to do — to find a secure source of income, to get by with less, to protect children during their most vulnerable ages, and to avoid being trapped in a hazardous situation in old age. More and more individuals will develop cooperative arrangements with others to make life better and more satisfying.

In short, the dwindling faith in government's ability to solve our problems (which we are already experiencing), will stimulate individual adaptation before it would otherwise be absolutely necessary, permitting a more orderly pace of change and more time to investigate alternatives.

CHAPTER II

An Ecological View of History

The isolation of knowledge within disciplines has one advantage: different perspectives and insights can be seen if one looks across the empty space from one discipline to another. There is much truth in the argument that each discipline is as much a point of view as it is a body of knowledge. History, and particularly the process by which fundamental changes occur, looks quite different when seen in an ecological way. The account here — of necessity brief and highly generalized — is meant to suggest the manner in which change can be expected to occur in the future by looking at cultural changes that have occurred in the past. There are many different interpretations of historical experience. What is important is the process by which an equilibrium evolves, and how it is broken.

The historian is interested in the great figures of the past — statesmen, generals, philosophers, discoverers; as well as the base figures: tyrants, conquerors, traitors — all the actors and their interplay. The cultural ecologist stands farther away and cannot discern the individual players; their accomplishments, good or bad, appear only as variations in the surface texture of each era. The cultural ecologist looks for the general topography and asks why the slope tends upward or downward. Surface events are interesting, but only as they reflect the powerful underlying forces that determine man's use of the environment and that lead to different methods of livelihood, larger populations, technological advance, or increased mobility. Anything that fundamentally changes the interrelationships between culture and the environment is of interest.

Ecological history is history from the ground up. It suggests that when the time is ripe, historical occurrences are virtually inevitable. The discovery of America was almost inevitable once the broad expansion of science, navigation, and maritime trade had reached a certain point; if Columbus had not done it, someone else soon would have. Luther simply made explicit the cultural gap that had appeared between the Renaissance church in Rome and the medieval church of northern Europe. Marx was only the most influential voice in a broad movement against the abuses of the factory owners during the Industrial Revolution. In recent times the pre-eminence of underlying forces is clearer still. The development of nuclear technology has occurred in virtually all countries that have the necessary technological sophistication and political will. The inventor is society as a whole rather than the individual. Are there at present no towering figures — either in this country or elsewhere — that can be said to be directing the course of events? I can think of none. Perhaps there never have been. The great leaders of the past were probably those who most clearly understood the trends of their times and were able to capitalize on them.

Our confidence in our ability to direct the course of events has been severely eroded by the experiences of the twentieth century. Several disastrous wars have occurred, against all efforts to prevent them, and even the United Nations has been almost totally unsuccessful in achieving the peaceful world that was its founding vision. We seem powerless to control crime, urban deterioration, overpopulation, the arms race, and nuclear proliferation. These experiences suggest that there is a grand dynamic in history that goes largely where it will and is highly resistant to efforts made to redirect it. Programs that try to counter it are unsuccessful, no matter how vigorously they are pursued, while programs that go with the grain of the times go smoothly and virtually fall into place.

Many of the changes stemming from resource scarcity will have this type of inexorability about them; they will shape our society whether we want them to or not, and no matter how hard we try to avoid them. In contrast to some social problems, which can be denied or suppressed, often for quite a long time, the shortage of essential raw materials will have a cold, hard effect on the functioning of our economy.

This does not mean we are helpless before the juggernaut of change. Even though there is little we can

do to influence the onset of scarcity in the years immediately ahead, in the long run there is a process at work
in our favor; it is the process of cultural evolution. Cultural evolution, when it has operated successfully, has
been able to make life good in the past no matter how
harsh the environmental circumstances; that is its
genius. But successful cultural evolution is by no
means assured. In the past, some societies have not survived, and others have evolved in unsatisfactory directions, into dead ends or traps, in much the same way
that industrial society would be trapped if it allowed its
basic resources to run out without making alternative
arrangements. How we respond to the depletion of
nonrenewable resources is not predetermined in any
way. Cultural evolution is inevitable, but its direction
is up to us.

By looking back at the halting process of cultural
evolution in the past, we can get some idea of the nature of the process — its pace and the way different
methods of livelihood have brought forth different
types of human behavior. The earthiness of the ecological perspective requires that we focus on the different
ways of making a living from the environment, and
how this has been integrated with, and reinforced by,
cultural inventions.

Our Genetic Heritage: Hunters and Gatherers

Whenever I hear someone say that because of our
modern consciousness the future will have to be some-

thing brand new (inferring that there is little we can learn from the past), I like to remind them that during the last 150,000 years the size of the human brain has not changed, nor has anything else about *Homo sapiens* changed except the superficial adaptation to different environments that we call race. Our technology has changed spectacularly and our numbers have grown huge, but our minds and our bodies operate the same ways as in ages past.

Homo sapiens has been a hunter and gatherer for 90 percent of his existence, and if to this period we add the era of pre-man, the figure rises to 99 percent of our ancestry. Because of this long evolutionary experience, hunting and gathering is the way of life for which we are genetically "wired," and it fits comfortably with our physical and psychological makeup. Our tendency has long been to regard this ancestry as primitive. Recently, books dealing with hunting and gathering societies have served to help counter this condescension toward "primitive" people, perhaps because civilization (in the original sense of the word, meaning urban-based societies) is no longer at war with hunters and gatherers for land and resources.[1] We no longer feel the need to picture them, as Thomas Hobbes did in the seventeenth century, as savages in a war of all against all. If there was such a war, we have won it, and there is now no danger in being generous to the vanquished. And even though the world population is now so great that there is no chance of returning to hunting and gathering as a method of livelihood, it is still useful to

understand this way of life because of the light it
throws on our genetic makeup.

In a fascinating article in *Scientific American,* "The
Origin of Society," anthropologist Marshall Sahlins
identifies what seems to be the most basic differences
between the simplest hunting and gathering societies
that still survive and the society of our closest animal
relatives, the primates.[2] Sahlins argues that the key difference is the control of sex. Among apes and mon-
keys, males compete with each other for females, and
so sex involves a great deal of conflict. This behavior
has survival value since the strongest males mate with
the females, and the offspring thus carry the genetic
material of the strongest male. But in human society
this advantage is foregone, and the sexual free-for-all
is constrained on all sides by taboos in order to encourage cooperation. The most important taboo is that
against incest, and its key cultural function is to create
harmony in the family. If parents and children competed for sexual favors, there would be continuous
tension in the family, and it could not function as a cooperative unit. The incest taboo also had the advantage of creating blood ties between separate families
in the tribe. Since marriage outside the family was
favored, blood ties would eventually spread widely
throughout the group. And since hunting and gathering societies were usually small, a tribal group soon
came to see all its members as having descended from
common ancestors. Such a view helped form a strong,
cohesive group. In this way, the competition of the

primate groups was replaced with cooperation and mutual aid. The phrase "survival of the fittest" is correct only up to a point; beyond that it should be "survival of the most cooperative." Richard Leakey makes this point very strongly in his book *Origins,* and demonstrates it by the progress early man made compared to his primate relatives.[3]

In early societies, hunting was man's work, and although it did not normally bring in as much food as the gathering done by women, it did serve to organize society and did so very satisfactorily. For one thing, hunting made sharing virtually inevitable. Because meat rotted quickly, a killed animal had to be divided and consumed before its value was lost. Hunting peoples characteristically feast after a successful hunt, and then enjoy themselves by relaxing, playing, telling stories, or recounting past hunts, until it is time for the next hunt. Hunters were blessed with all sorts of positive incentives to hunt; not only was hunting challenging and exciting, but the successful hunter also enjoyed the deference accorded to him when he was able to give away more meat than he received from others. Moreover, the hunter was free from internal conflict since to do what was most enjoyable and in one's own best interest — to kill animals and give away the meat — was also in the group's interest. Selflessness and selfishness were satisfied by the same act. There was still competitiveness, but it was of a positive nature.

In addition, the best hunter often became the leader of the band, although not always. The leader, in any case, was not elected and usually had little or no authority; his main role was to advise. He gained his position by giving the advice that was considered the best and so was most often accepted. Among the Shoshoni, the name for the leader was "the talker," and for the Eskimos it is "he who thinks." The other leader was the shaman — the witch doctor in Tarzan terminology — a function accorded to the individual who had the best psychological insights; who could give sound advice on matters of the mind and spirit; who knew about the tribal spirits and rituals; and who could recite the band's myths and knew its history and stories.

The other factor that was instrumental in giving hunting and gathering societies their attractive characteristics was that they were almost always nomadic. To move regularly meant that personal possessions had to be kept to a minimum, leaving no chance that individuals would compete for status through accumulation of material things. The readiness of hunters and gatherers to give away what they had and the poor care given to their possessions were regularly reported by visitors to tribal groups. With so much leisure, there was plenty of time to make new things, a pleasurable pastime; and they used materials that were common to them: bone, sinews, skins, and wood. It was only in rare cases that nomadism was not necessary, such as around the mouths of rivers in the Pacific Northwest, where a steady supply of seafood as well as freshwater fish from the rivers permitted settled communities. The settled affluence of the Indians of the Pacific

Northwest led them to the custom of the potlatch, in which individuals competed to become wealthy enough to give away more than others could return to them. They still shared, but with a vengeance; it was more like the economic warfare of our own society.

Each tribal group came to terms with its environment and learned when animals should not be killed, what plants were edible, and how to stay comfortable during different seasons. The spirits tended to keep each group in its own territory; if they ventured outside its boundaries, the spirits were unfamiliar and possibly dangerous, and the shaman was less sure of being able to deal with them. American Indians always resisted being moved away from their homelands, knowing that their chances of finding enough food to survive in an alien environment were slim, and that it probably would mean slow starvation. Time and again they would return to their ancestral lands and face death rather than die slowly in a foreign place. The Eskimos love the Arctic and the Bushmen love the desert as much as other hunters and gatherers loved more benevolent landscapes. Warfare was rare except in societies that became culturally trapped in it, as when warfare was necessary to gain manhood or high status, or when an equilibrium was upset, such as after the horse was introduced on the Great Plains. But this was unusual, and most reports are of gentle, peaceable people.

Controlling population seems to have been the most unpleasant task of hunters and gatherers. Migration,

as a response to overpopulation, was rarely possible
and then only from the periphery of occupied areas.
Even then it was hazardous: little food could be carried
along and new territory might provide little to eat; or
the good lands reached might already be occupied by
others. Migration was a desperate, temporary step,
and sooner or later it would be necessary to maintain
the group's population within the bounds of the environment's carrying capacity. It must have been a heavy
burden, however, for a parent to expose a child because it could not be supported, or for men and
women to endure long periods of sexual abstinence following the birth of a baby. But these sacrifices were
found to be absolutely essential, otherwise the group
found itself living on the edge of survival, having to eat
starvation food such as leaves and bark, and watching
sickness and death hover over the band. Population
control was essential for the good life.

Beyond this painful obligation, hunters and gatherers seemed to be remarkably happy, easygoing people.
They were able to enjoy leisure and still rise to the
challenge of the hunt, and they had the capacity to
sustain themselves by using only simple technology,
something few of us can say these days. The books writ-
ten about hunters and gatherers by outsiders who had
the opportunity to live with them while their way of life
was still intact are inspiring reading, and the reports
confirm the good fit that millions of years of evolution
produced.[4]

The Fall from the Garden: Agriculture

Depending on one's attitude toward progress, it could be said either that the single greatest achievement of the human race was made by women, or that all our problems can be blamed on them since there is every reason to believe that women invented agriculture over a long period of time. Just as women were prohibited from hunting by taboos, men generally did not gather plant foods. Women must have always been trying to find new ways to use plants since if this could be done the carrying capacity of the environment would be increased, and there could be a respite from the unpleasant task of population control.

The seeds of wild grasses were difficult to utilize. They had husks that had to be removed, in itself a difficult job; and then some way had to be found to cook the hard, nutlike grains so they could be digested. Sometimes they were parched on hot rocks, rather as popcorn is made; and sometimes they were allowed to soak in water, or hot rocks were added to cook them a bit to soften them for easier digestion. It is believed that the making of beer was stumbled onto in this way, and that it preceded the making of bread. But in both cases, the natural yeast in grains, when properly incubated, was adequate to produce beer and bread.[5]

Even though it was slow, time-consuming work to harvest the grains, thresh them, and make them edible, they were a highly nutritious food. If only one food was available to live on, the grains would be the best choice. They are closer to providing a balanced diet than any other single food.[6] Grain not only contains the embryo of the young plant — the germ — but also all the nutrients and energy the young plant needs until it produces its own leaves and roots that enable it to grow on its own. That which sustains the young plant sustains us also. The grains have one other essential advantage; unlike most other foods they can be stored over long periods of time to provide an assured food supply as a protection against times of scarcity.

But the using of grains did not amount to agriculture. The growing of food probably required several thousand years to develop. The first cultivation of grains seems to have occurred in the Zagros Mountains above the Tigris and Euphrates valleys, where wild wheat and barley can still be found growing. As with so many other foods, women must have found that if they collected all the grains off the plants there would be no crop the next year; the spirits punished them for being greedy. But even removing part of the crop of seeds gave an advantage to competing nonfood species of plants, so these competing plants were pulled out whenever possible; the first weeding. Perhaps then it was noticed that seeds that happened to get into the refuse heaps at the edge of camp did very well. This suggested that cleared, disturbed ground was good for growing grains and that fertilization was helpful too. The cultivators may have found that areas of loosened, cleared earth could be left around camps. They may have dug camp refuse into the areas and scattered some seeds there, so that when they returned to the camp next time there would be a supply of grain available. The final step was to plant a bigger field, stay by it all the time, watch over it, and build a permanent camp.

The men, of course, would have had nothing to do with this if they had a choice, but their choices became very constricted. As more food was slowly obtained by agriculture and more children could be supported, the men probably found that hunting was deteriorating. More hunters had to share the animals that were available. It become apparent that if animals were to remain a part of men's lives they had to be protected from other hunters and herded from one feeding place to another. At this stage a very painful decision had to be made; either to settle down to agriculture — in effect to do women's work — or to attempt to migrate somewhere so that men could continue a way of life based on animals. One theory is that in the splitting of the ways, the spirited ones took their animals and went north to the vast open space of central Asia and became herders. After domesticating the horse, they became the mounted warriors that periodically poured down into settled areas to the south, from Europe to Asia, and raided the people they considered debased, because the men did "women's work" and deserved such a fate.[7]

But it was agriculture that led to the revolutionary changes. The oldest permanent agricultural settlements that have been found date from around 7000

B.C. in the hills of Iraq.[8] Living in settlements permitted a number of advances that were not possible for
nomads; permanent houses, pottery, and looms all
quickly appeared. As the agricultural settlements expanded — for now there was no reason to restrain
population growth — they moved farther down the
hills. As they moved to the level land of the Tigris
River Valley, the weather got hotter and modest irrigation systems became necessary to divert water from
streams to the fields; but the result was higher crop
yield and reduced risk of crop failure from inadequate
rainfall.

However, as agricultural communities appeared,
their stored grain supplies became very tempting to
bandits who could make an easy living by raiding
farmers and taking their grain. The farmers were de-
fenseless against this plague, especially when the raiders
were mounted on horses and carried spears with
bronze tips. The actual process by which agricultur-
ists lost their freedom is not known, but it is possible
that they formed their own defensive units, only to
have their own guards — once trained and outfitted —
turn on them and demand more and more tribute,
forcing the farmers to work harder and harder in order
to satisfy their own defenders. Perhaps a chief guard
declared himself king, built himself a fortified city,
lived off the sweat of the farmers, and occupied himself by making war on neighboring areas. If so, he remained interested in agriculture, however, because if
he could increase its productivity there would be a

larger surplus to support his activities. He would be able to maintain a larger army and obtain more bronze for weapons and decorations for his women and his palace. He might have also patronized practitioners of science, math, and the arts. Astronomy was especially valuable in order to know the correct time to plant. But as Kenneth Boulding has remarked, early civilization was largely a protection racket. The evidence suggests that civilization originated only in those areas surrounded by hostile environments which did not permit enslaved peoples to escape.[9]

For the common man, the whole process of change from hunting and gathering to agriculture must have been a disaster. He went from being a proud member of an independent band of hunters that was intricately adapted to the environment to being a farmer tied to the soil, doing hard, boring work. Furthermore, he was exploited by tax collectors and mounted warriors. The Biblical legend of the expulsion from the Garden of Eden seems clearly to describe the invention of agriculture. The tree of knowledge was the knowledge of agriculture; "The tree was good for food," and the woman took the first step — "She took the fruit thereof and did eat" (Genesis 3:60). The penalty was expulsion from the Garden and "In the sweat of thy face shalt thou eat bread" (Genesis 3:19). Most important, it was irreversible. Once the knowledge had been gained and populations had risen above the carrying capacity of the environment of the hunter and gatherer, there was no turning back. The expulsion from the Garden was

final. "The Lord sent him forth from the Garden of
Eden, to till the ground from which he was taken"
(Genesis 3:23). Mankind would henceforth live in an
intimate relationship with the soil.

Making Agriculture Fit: The Elaboration of Culture

We are familiar with the achievements of the earliest
civilizations which emerged after 4000 B.C. When one
kingdom succeeded in conquering a number of others
in the Tigris and Euphrates valleys, vast surpluses
could be brought together in one spot. With threatening armies largely destroyed or incorporated under
one king, these surpluses could safely be diverted to
other purposes, such as architecture, public administration, metallurgy, expanded irrigation systems,
trade, as well as the arts and sciences. Success bred
more success; each development increased the power
and prestige of the ruler; patronage of the intellectual
elite paid off as it has ever since. The ruler had all sorts
of positive incentives to maintain a bone-crushing level
of oppression and to take as much as he could from the
farmers and artisans. In some favored areas, the surpluses grew so large that monumental structures such
as the Pyramids, the Tower of Babel, and the Great
Wall of China could be built.

It was an age of excess not unlike the early Industrial
Revolution. Self-centered individualism was the style
of the powerful, and the common people had little
choice but to get by as well as they could. In both

periods, the amount of work accomplished boggles the mind, especially given the primitive tools used. There was no effective restraining force on the powerful, who could coerce the weak into doing whatever was wanted. In both eras, work was turned into a tribulation. It was long and tedious and provided little beyond subsistence. And there was no incentive to share as there had been among hunting peoples.

Following the invention of agriculture and the appearance of the first civilizations, the empires grew one after another as the balance of power shifted: Sumeria, Egypt, Assyria, Babylon, Persia, Greece, and Rome. And even though the records of the small, peaceful groups of people who were overrun by the conquerors are virtually nonexistent (only the Jews have preserved much of the history of their experiences under the Roman occupation), there can be little doubt that it was a hard time. Slavery was the rule in the capitals of the empires. The main alternative was to become a soldier, which enabled a slave who played the ruler's game to move upward and improve his status.

There is little doubt that all through the early civilizations there must have been efforts to make life better for the common people, but these efforts were probably not effective enough to overcome the very clear advantages that accrued to rulers who maintained their power by taking as much as possible from the people under their sway. To rationalize their behavior, rulers could point to the unstable balance of power between opposing empires and say that a country's whole oppressive system was necessary to preserve its subjects from other military powers (an analogy with the present). Yet, culture slowly did achieve a basis on which to restrain the exploitation of the common people by rulers, and it probably came through the moderating force of religion.

The sixth century B.C. was a remarkable century in retrospect; it was a period of time that produced a large percentage of the world's great religious figures: Buddha, Confucius, Lao-tze, Zoroaster, and the last of the major prophets of Israel. It is this very confluence that suggests that after a long struggle, the tide had finally begun to turn against exploitation. For to restrain rulers, religion not only had to threaten them with the punishment of hell, or something similar, it also had to achieve its effects over large areas *at roughly the same time* so as to maintain political and military equilibrium.

The military leaders were not likely to be the types to tremble at the thought of a penalty in the afterlife; still, they could not know for sure. Further, if new religious beliefs were being widely accepted and the ruler refused to accept them or tried to repress them, then he had to face the prospect of a populace broadly opposed to him and so risk rebellion. The wiser course of action seemed to be to accept the religion, expecially if traditional enemies were becoming less dangerous because of the spread of religion as well, and to try and turn it to advantage. Religion became part of a ruler's strategy for maintaining political control. At least it allowed into politics the restraining force of religious ethics.

Today, government and business compete for the right to organize society — as pure capitalism or pure socialism; in the past, government and religion competed for ascendency. The best situation seems to be when the two opposing forces are equally powerful, and both have to act with care and discretion in order to maintain public support for what they do. Religion constricted the absolute authority of monarchs and forced them to worry about public opinion; they were no longer free to do only what was in their own best interests. Religion maintained its public base by looking out for the interests of the common people, providing for their well-being and enriching their lives, while trying to stay in the good graces of the ruler. It could be an awkward position, but it did serve to integrate society. For example, during the later Dark Ages the Catholic church conferred on rulers the divine right of kings in return for the king's acceptance of the moral requirements of the church, a state of affairs that was successful in maintaining a balance of power for centuries until the times of Henry VIII and the Reformation.

As the role of religion in cultural evolution expanded, the nature of the world's cultures changed too. They not only became richer and more complex, but very diverse as well, as they evolved in different ways in different environments. The Aryan invaders,

who conquered India some two thousand years before
Christ and set up a caste system to maintain their
dominant position, saw India evolve in a distinctly
Eastern way. Its resistance to invaders became insignificant, but its culture was powerful enough to absorb
conquerors into the ongoing life in India. In China,
the system of manners and morals that Confucius established contributed to a culture that maintained its
continuity longer than any other country. Europe was
a backward region until relatively late, and the Catholic church had to capitalize on a dying Roman Empire
and the breakdown into the Dark Ages before it could
get a strong foothold. But slowly, the great diversity of
European traditional society evolved, both in the
heartland of Europe — Italy, France, England, and
Germany — and in the peripheries of the continent,
from Scandinavia to Spain, Greece, and Eastern
Europe.

Out of the youthful excesses of civilization, cultural
evolution slowly produced relatively stable, rich cultures. The general disequilibrium caused by the invention of agriculture was greatly reduced, and the lives of
the common people were improved.

Agricultural skills also developed, especially in areas
where long periods of habitation had permitted the
slow accumulation of ecological experience. In parts of
China, rice has been cultivated on the same land for
four thousand years, and in many other areas human
cultivation has actually improved soils by draining
them, aerating them, building terraces, and over-

coming mineral deficiencies.[10] But this has not been the case everywhere. The first agriculturalists in the Zagros Mountains above the Tigris and Euphrates valleys did not learn fast enough, and today the hills are largely denuded of soil and thinly populated. The irrigation systems of the Tigris and Euphrates valleys were made useless by the sedimentation washed down from the hills, and excessive irrigation and poor drainage led to salination of the soils. The hills of the Mediterranean were cleared of their trees, overgrazed, and allowed to erode. Everywhere in the contemporary world, the pressure of population is leading to the expansion of agriculture in areas that are unsuitable and it is almost certain to be destructive, and thus temporary. There is still a long way to go before ultimate stability is achieved — the kind of stability that is based on long experience in using the land without undermining its productivity. This has been made impossible, at least for the time being, by a vast new kind of instability on a scale never before seen on the earth.

Renewed Disequilibrium: The Modern Era

The age of discovery provides a perfect example of how disequilibrium with all its far-flung consequences can be triggered. Once the initial discovery of the New World had been followed by conquest, and the gold started flowing into Spain, it was inevitable that other European countries with the capacity to do so would join in the scramble, even if it meant plundering Spanish galleons in order to get started, as was the case with England. To do otherwise — not to join in the free-for-all — would have meant relative decline for any abstaining country.

The riches flowing into Europe produced a great increase in the money supply but little increase in goods, and the predictable result was inflation. This situation impoverished peasants and nobles alike but made the bankers of Florence and Venice wealthy enough to exhibit their new affluence by patronizing the arts. The church in Rome became caught up in the spirit of the times, and the pope became a Renaissance prince. Not surprisingly, northern Christendom refused to be a party to these excesses. In reacting, the Protestants threw out much of what was good in Catholicism along with the bad. The stage was thus set for centuries of religious conflict, including some of the bloodiest wars in European history.

In India, the British East India Company stirred up internal strife to help establish its control, and then expropriated enough precious metals, jewels, silks, and spices to make London the wealthiest city in the world. China was more difficult to penetrate, but finally trade was initiated, assisted by gunboats and opium. When China tried to outlaw opium and burned the warehouses where it was stored, the action was considered enough justification for Europeans to come in and take larger and larger "trade concessions" in order to protect "free trade." Africa was left relatively alone for a while since it did not have any obvious wealth to lure adventurers; to be poor was the greatest protection, for a time at least. But when Europeans, and by this time Americans, had worked through most of the highly valued prizes to be obtained from the rest of the world, there were only human beings left in which to "trade" profitably. The slave trade took some 40 or 50 million people from Africa, but only one-third ever reached the New World alive. It is interesting to speculate how we would have dealt with the Indians of North America if this country had been as densely populated with natives as was Africa. Of the 1 to 2 two million Indians estimated to have been in America at the time of the first white settlements, only 25,731 survived in 1860.[11]

While Europe's museums and palaces filled up with the art treasures taken from the rest of the world, its own internal disruption continued. After centuries of religious wars following the Reformation, European peasantry then had to face the slow undermining of their livelihood as the structure of the medieval world was slowly dismantled. Calvin's emphasis on economic success as an indication of whether one was predestined for heaven (a belief that is hard to find much basis for in the Bible) had removed the medieval restraints on the acquisition of wealth and replaced them by a strong incentive to make money. In effect, Calvin had contrived a device to permit the commercial classes of northern Europe to do what they wanted to do anyway — to get involved in the economic activity stimulated by the age of discovery. But since the Calvinists did not approve of consuming the wealth earned

— that was too much like the church in Rome — there was nothing else to do with it but to reinvest it. The result was capitalism, the economic system by which profits were reinvested rather than spent.[12]

This system soon generated so much economic momentum that it left Calvinism behind. As the free trade movement gained the ascendency, the medieval restraints on economic activity were removed. The enclosure movement transferred common lands into private holdings; the market was allowed to determine price and wages; guilds were disbanded; and in 1870 the Corn Laws were repealed in England, and cheap imported American grains flooded in and ruined small farmers and landed aristocrats alike. Power shifted irrevocably to the commercial classes. The choices for people in the villages were reduced to being landless agricultural laborers at less than subsistence wages, or going to work for twelve or fourteen hours a day in the factories of the industrial towns and cities. A good many peasants in the world today face the same choices except that now there are fewer factory jobs, emigration is not possible, and there is the added affliction of overpopulation.

We have been able to avoid feelings of guilt about all these brutal changes because of the belief that change was bringing something better to people, no matter how painful the process. The Puritan factory owners told their suffering workers that their misery was God's stimulus to make them improve themselves. (Not only were factory workers exploited, but they were told it was good for them!) Our forebears were confident enough about what they were doing to disrupt other cultures in order to let their own religion and economics in. Whether such changes were actually an improvement or not, only time can tell, but, there is no denying that throughout this period of history we have tended to see the worst in other peoples and consistently pictured them in negative terms. The American Indians were savages who were killing innocent settlers. It was necessary to see other people as pagans and barbarians in order to justify treating them as such.

The Prospects Ahead

We have made a great deal of technological and economic progress in the last two centuries, since the Industrial Revolution and the age of colonial empires. In the terms of cultural evolution, however, industrial society is still young and raw. It can be expected to mature, and, with enough time, cultural evolution could do for our society what it did for early agricultural civilization. It could slowly bring about far better ways of utilizing the technology of modern society, ways that have a benign effect on individuals, families, communities, and the environment.

All this is possible if — and this is the rub — enough time is available. Cultural evolution is a slow, halting process. Thousands of years were necessary to transform early agricultural civilizations, with all their exploitations, into the great array of traditional societies

that occupied the earth at the start of the age of discovery. We know virtually nothing about the process
by which hunters and gatherers built their highly satis-
factory way of life, but we do know that they had hundreds of thousands of years for the task, if they needed
it. Such spans of time are not available to us. It may be
argued that cultural evolution today is much faster,
and that we will not need so much time to soften the
raw edges of urban industrial society. But the counter-
argument can also be made that contemporary
changes may not be productive ones, in the evolutionary sense; we may, in fact, be throwing out valuable
aspects of our own heritage that are the product of a
long evolutionary experience, rather than creating
anything that will turn out to be "progress" from the
vantage point of the future.

The question of whether modern society is or is not
moving in constructive directions is academic; it hardly makes much difference. Whether urban industrial
society is advancing or decaying, in the cultural sense,
is overshadowed by the fact that in the *material sense* it
has passed its youth. It is now middle-aged and beginning to show signs of old age, and loss of vitality. The
resources simply are not available to maintain industrial civilization while the processes of cultural evolution
transform it into a rich and satisfying way of life. Our
personal feelings about modern life are almost beside
the point. Increasingly, the situation regarding resources will determine the shape of the future more
than our political, economic, or social aspirations.

CHAPTER III

Advancing Technology, Declining Resources

The history of resource use since the beginning of the Industrial Revolution is a fascinating one. It is also a perfect example of the kind of history that is of far more interest to the cultural ecologist than to the historian. To someone with an ecological perspective, it ties all sorts of basic things together: new tools developed; new methods of livelihood; changes in settlement patterns; plus all the different forms of human behavior that were called forth. All of these things, and many more, would not have occurred without advances in the utilization of previously unused natural resources.

Resource scarcity is not new to industrial society. Although we may look back covetously on the high-grade resources that we have used up, in most cases they were not put to use until traditional materials became scarce, and only then after some form of technological advance was achieved. The resources were not just lying there on the ground waiting to be used. It was necessary to find ways to wrest them from the earth and to put them to use. The striking thing about this process is how frequently technological advance, once it was initiated, went far beyond resolving the original shortage and radically extended the resources available to an expanding industrial civilization. There are enough examples of scarcity averted by technological advance to make understandable the expectation among many people today that this is the way it will always be. It could be a dangerous assumption.

The "Easy" Times

The virgin resources first exploited in the eighteenth and nineteenth centuries were not seen as a wonderful boon by the workers caught up in the Industrial Revolution, yet their development and utilization contributed greatly to our present way of life. A number of the most difficult, even desperate, steps that unlocked the industrial niche were made in England and were brought to this country ready to use.

One of the reasons London became Europe's largest city in the sixteenth century was that it was able to escape the constraint imposed by the scarcity of firewood by using coal. Found on the beaches below the eroding headlands of northeastern England, these "sea coals" were first used in medieval times, even though wood was considered the superior fuel. Coal was smelly and smoky, and it necessitated the addition of chimneys to dwellings; prior to that, smoke was simply allowed to escape through a hole in the roof.[1] The location of coal deposits near the coast made it possible to ship coal to London by water, the only feasible mode of transportation at that time. As wood became progressively scarce, the use of coal expanded and spread to other English cities. A major industry developed.

England is a wet country, and as coal production expanded, the coal mines almost immediately went down below the water table. Crude pumps were used to drain the mines and were usually powered by horses. This was expensive as well as inefficient, and a number of generally unsuccessful efforts were made to develop a "fire" pump that used the material being mined as a source of energy. Not until 1762 did Watt's reciprocating steam engine appear with its wide usefulness. Think of the changes that it triggered in only a little over two hundred years. Steam rapidly replaced water power as the motive force behind a significantly expanded Industrial Revolution.

Until the eighteenth century, iron was made with charcoal, putting a heavy drain on England's forests. Numerous early efforts to substitute coke made from coal were unsuccessful. The demand for charcoal compounded the problem already created by England's growing population and the demands of its navy for ship's timbers. Through careful selection of the coal used, Abraham Derby finally succeeded in producing iron made from coke, increasing England's capacity for making iron by a factor of several thousands. Iron and steel became plentiful enough and cheap enough to replace wood in England's navy, and wood for building was replaced by brick from coal-fired ovens. A whole new era was opening up; the niche of industrial society was being discovered by the first tentative explorers, a process which would soon turn into a flood tide.

With the expansion of production, transportation increased and roads rapidly deteriorated. Wagon wheels cut deeper and deeper into the dirt tracks that were called roads at the time, so that after a rain they frequently became impassible. The number of horses needed for transportation and the amount of land to feed them was also becoming a problem. By 1800 the horse tax was paid for 1.35 million animals in England, a number which required an estimated 5.4 million acres of agricultural land for feed — some 14 percent of the entire area of England and Wales and a much higher percentage of the agricultural lands.[2] Track-mounted wagons had already been used to reduce the drag on wagon wheels, and the addition of steam power was inevitable, occurring first in 1802. With the railroad, speeds and payloads increased immensely, ultimately making the horse a plaything of the wealthy and releasing millions of acres of land for food production.

In England, every step on the way toward a modern industrial society was resisted by the forces of tradition, which the great majority of people endorsed. The initiation of the market economy was a particular source of strife since it required the elimination of all contractual relations between individuals so that the market for labor could operate freely. Traditional allegiances to family, village, or guild had to be destroyed. To create a class of mobile laborers, it was necessary to destroy the feudal system, to force peasants off land to which they had common rights (in many cases to tear down entire villages), and to leave a single option — the labor market in the new industrial system. This process is vividly described by Karl Polanyi in *The Great Transformation*.[3]

In America, by contrast, the availability of land and the limited social constraints of a frontier society enabled us to develop without such traditional hindrances and to emerge as a clearer example of a modern, free enterprise society. We had our scarcities, too, but they were not as critical as the earlier ones that England had surmounted. For example, the search for a fuel for lighting led from tallow candles to whale oil, which eventually caused the virtual disappearance of the whales from the Atlantic Coast. A new fuel was needed. Petroleum had been known for a long time, but it was the discovery that kerosene could be made from oil that made a well drilled in Pennsylvania in 1859 famous; it was the first oil well that was a commercial success. Kerosene took over the lighting market and led to the demise of the New England whaling industry. The whales had a reprieve, for the time being anyway.

The success stories, a continuing string of them, have followed us into the present, and a number are almost certain to extend into the future. The internal combustion engine was developed to take advantage of

the highly concentrated energy in petroleum-based
fuels. Light and capable of high speeds, this engine
quickly displaced the steam monsters. In agriculture, a
progression of machines, powered first by horses, then
by steam, and finally by internal combustion engines,
radically reduced the need for manual labor. The limited supplies of agricultural nitrogen from guano deposits were supplemented and then replaced by nitrogen produced from natural gas. When the high-grade
iron ores of the Mesabi Range in Minnesota were
worked out, a low-grade ore called taconite, which was
available in vast quantities, was made usable by bene-
ficiation technology, a process that concentrates the
ore without an increase in price. It is as if each potential scarcity led to the uncovering of an even more
plentiful resource.

In some cases, errors were made in assessing our natural resources, thereby creating unnecessary fears of
depletion and scarcity. Timber supplies at the turn of
the century provide a good example. Theodore Roose-
velt's conservation movement was, in part, a response
to the fear that timber supplies were rapidly being depleted. With the eastern forests logged or cleared for
farming and the forests of the Great Lakes states cut
rapidly and wastefully to provide cheap lumber for the
westward expansion, it seemed that the only remaining
good resources were those of the Pacific Northwest.
Yet the expected timber famine never arrived. In retrospect, it is easy to see why. The volume of timber in
the vast Douglas fir forests of Oregon and Washington

were much larger than anyone realized, but more important, regrowth of logged-over land everywhere was faster than expected. Second-growth timber can often be harvested after fifty years, and in even less time in warmer areas such as the southeast, where forestry has expanded rapidly on soils too poor for agriculture. Yet even this error had its benefits. The fear of a timber famine helped to establish the U.S. Forest Service — some skeptics even suggested that the famine was part of the strategy to establish a federal forestry agency. True or not, the Forest Service was able to restrain wasteful logging practices, reduce fires, and assure better second growth of this renewable resource. Public disgust with the way forests were being turned into fence posts eventually led to the establishment of national parks intended to preserve irreplaceable landscapes of national significance, an idea that has spread worldwide.

The Pleasures and Pitfalls of Abundance

Our history is really one of abundance, not scarcity.[4] There are many illustrations of the pure glory of having an abundance of resources. Land is the classic example, the one resource that this country had in true abundance and the resource above all others that permitted the freedom which we value so much.

In Europe, laws of primogeniture were required to stop the continued division of land between sons, a fragmentation that led to smaller farms and more impoverished farmers. Under the laws of primogeniture, property was willed intact to the eldest son. England especially found it a good policy to force younger sons to set out "to make their fortunes," to man privateers, to colonize new territories, and to initiate commercial ventures in the growing towns and cities. Primogeniture was a perfect device to increase national wealth and power, to force Englishmen to grasp the opportunities that technological advance was creating. But for most it meant being uprooted from the only life they knew, to become landless laborers, foot soldiers, beggars, or "hands" in the new mills.

For people to whom ownership of land determined one's wealth and status, it is easy to understand the attraction of North America, a huge, fertile continent, wide open for settlement. The Homestead Act was as logical in this country as primogeniture was in Europe. In the land-rich United States, governmental generosity was virtually required if the land was to be settled and put to use, and the Indians were to be subdued. The only obstacle to the Homestead Act was the eastern manufacturing interests, who did not want to lose their cheap labor supply. But by 1862, the East needed the West's support on the slavery issue, and the Homestead Act was passed and signed into law by President Lincoln. Homesteaders not only enjoyed 160 acres of free land, but schools were also funded from the public domain. Two sections of land, 640 acres each, were set aside for schools in each township of thirty-six sections, to be sold as needed for education in the township.

The land-grant colleges were funded this way, too, as were canals and the early roads. It was certainly a far nicer way to finance government facilities than by levying taxes to pay for them.

In a similar way, national parks were established out of the public domain by a vote of Congress and a stroke of the president's pen. It was much easier than having to find the money to purchase them from unwilling landowners, as must be done today. The Redwood National Park, as it was established in 1968, required $190 million to purchase a paltry 28,000 acres of land, much of it logged-over, and another $359 million in 1978 when it was expanded by 48,000 acres. It offers a poor comparison with Yellowstone, in which 2.2 million acres of untouched wilderness were set aside without spending a dime. At the time Congress grumbled about spending money to station a few soldiers in Yellowstone to watch over it.

The 160-acre landholding available under the Homestead Act was a king-sized farm in the nineteenth century, more than a man and his family could effectively utilize. But the early settlers worked hard, prospered, built substantial homes and barns, and shipped their products to the East Coast on the rapidly expanding railroad system, much of it going on to Europe by steamship (there to undermine the livelihood of farmers carefully tending a few acres). Transportation technology had arrived just in time to effectively distribute the American agricultural products to markets worldwide. So far, so good. But at this point, the pitfalls of abundance began to appear. The same industrial technology soon showed its other face. As farm production increased, demand became insufficient to take all the crops that could be produced, and prices fell. This is the classic problem of abundance — overproduction and falling prices. For producers, the trick was to find some way to limit producing to a level the market will take at a good price. But the immigrant farmers, coming from land-poor Europe, had eyes only for the deep, black soil. As more virgin land was brought into production, prices fell further. To prop up their falling incomes, farmers desperately tried to increase their production — only to see a further price depression. Farmers were never able to organize themselves well enough to withhold their products from the market, as could other industries that were not characterized by so many small producers.

As farm income fell, the value of land fell also, and it soon became uneconomical for a farmer to care for his land properly. At times, the value of land fell to only a few dollars an acre, and it made no sense to spend much effort or money to care for it. Especially under the Homestead Act, there was a tendency to start again farther west, to take a new piece of land and "high grade" it — take the best timber or soil fertility out of it — and then move on again.

The opportunity to keep moving in this way, leaving the used-up land behind, is one of the most unfortunate consequences of abundance. It has contributed to both a transitoriness in America and to poor husbandry. The traditions in Europe were quite different. There, the landowner was continuously concerned about the care of his small piece of land since his well-being and that of his children depended on its productivity. Even today, the countryside of Europe is well lived in and well cared for. In this country, on the other hand, we still have a tendency to run away from our problems. The flight to the suburbs can be seen as another in a long series of escapes to avoid social and economic problems. Abundance has permitted us to do this.

Falling farm income ironically led to the reduction of soil erosion in an entirely unexpected way. As farm income declined, farmers inevitably became more and more preoccupied with the problems of economic survival. The efforts of the Soil Conservation Service to persuade farmers to build check dams or to take other erosion control steps generally failed, except when the farmers were paid by the government to do the work on their own land. Income was what was needed, whatever the source. So when the government, as part of a whole range of programs designed to reduce agricultural surpluses, decided to pay farmers not to produce crops under the Soil Bank Program, the farmers responded eagerly. Naturally, they decided to take the poorest, most erosion-prone land out of production. The healing powers of nature were allowed to take their course, and erosion was reduced significantly by a program designed for a totally different objective.

If anyone had suggested to the prosperous farmers of
a century ago that rural areas would be largely depopulated during the twentieth century, they would have
found it unimaginable. It would be like suggesting to
urban residents today that a hundred years from now
our cities will be largely depopulated. Americans
spend a smaller share of their income for food than do
the people of any other country, but one of the consequences has been the progressive depopulation of rural
areas. They have been transformed into efficient but
dehumanized agricultural landscapes. The young
people have been able to leave without much difficulty, but older people have had to face the decision of
accepting poverty rather than uprooting themselves
from the places they feel accustomed to. One of the
most disturbing aspects of many rural areas today is
the atmosphere of old age, loneliness, and poverty,
against a backdrop of vast fields and a few metal sheds
with big machines and very few workers. It is strange
the way resource abundance works on a land.

Abundance caused its problems with oil and natural
gas too. Even though many uses for petroleum quickly
developed — paving roads, firing boilers, and heating
homes, in addition to lighting — production soon exceeded demand, particularly after the huge eastern
Texas oil fields were discovered in the 1920s. The oil
industry developed under the "law of capture," which
meant that if an owner did not pump oil from under his own land his neighbor was likely to remove it
for him. This virtually assured rapid pumping, and time

and again the market was flooded and prices dropped to almost nothing, unless a tycoon such as John D. Rockefeller controlled the market in a region and charged whatever he wanted. Restrictions that limited the rate at which a field could be pumped were finally instituted in the 1930s. Since this regulation protected the industry from overproduction and thus increased profits, it was readily accepted.

For a long time natural gas was considered a useless byproduct of oil production, a highly explosive one that had to be flared, instead of being allowed to drift away when it came up with the oil. Of course, it was technically possible to use natural gas as a fuel, but it was too bulky to transport by rail or truck. Not until advances were made in pipeline technology, especially during World War II, did it become feasible to transport such gas to markets efficiently. But sufficient consumption had to be guaranteed before financing could be obtained to build pipelines, and this was done by offering long-term contracts for gas at prices that were cheap enough to encourage industries to convert to gas from other forms of energy. These contracts were to come back to haunt the gas pipeline companies later when low gas prices generated more demand than could be met, especially when air pollution restrictions caused a broad shift from coal and oil to gas. In the meantime, in a case brought by consumer groups in 1954, the Supreme Court ruled that prices for gas had to be set on the basis of the cost of production. Since gas rarely needs to be pumped from the ground and

does not require refining as oil does, this court ruling
caused gas to be the least expensive fossil fuel. This ruling meant, in effect, that the resource itself is deemed
to have no value, only the handling of it. There could
be no better illustration of our acceptance of abundance as the order of things.

But times are changing. The problem now is not depressed prices but rising prices, especially for nonrenewable resources. If lower prices are characteristic of
abundance, high prices are characteristic of scarcity.
Speculators are well aware of this; they look for things
that are fixed in supply and for which demand is increasing. The best investments in recent years, those
for which prices have risen the fastest — art, antiques,
and land — all reflect this perfectly.

Nonrenewable resources are also fixed in supply,
and demand has been increasing for many years. On
the basis of these two factors alone, it might be concluded that prices will inevitably continue to rise. But
with resources, technology must be brought into the
frame of reference. It is always possible that new ways
will be found to provide our resource needs — to use
previously unusable resources, to work low-grade ores,
to find substitutes for scarce materials, or to extend the
usefulness of existing resources by improving the efficiency with which they are used. Ideally, technologies
will be found to utilize renewable resources in lieu of
declining nonrenewable resources. If technological advances overcome approaching scarcities, the upward
price trend will be weakened. Technology thus as-

sumes a key role in the assessment of natural resources. In the next decades, technology will play an important part in determining the prices we pay for most things. In the long run, it will determine what life will be like when the inevitable transition to renewable resources takes place. Just as important, technology will determine how long it will be before this transition will occur.

The very rapid rate of research and development in recent times is starting to produce the first vague outlines of this future — what technology will be able to do and what it will not be able to do. The final results are speculative, but more and more it appears that the prospects for sustaining a high-level, industrial society are declining, while the prospects for a simple, decentralized way of life are good. The renewable resources and the simple technology to utilize them are available if we are willing to accept them and the frugal life they can support.

Let us now examine directly the situation regarding resources, and the help we can expect from technology.

Outlook on Resources: Minerals, Agriculture, and Energy

Real-estate agents are fond of saying that there are three main things to look for in choosing a home; neighborhood, neighborhood, and neighborhood. With raw materials, the three factors are energy,

energy, and energy. With sufficient energy, we will be free to use our technological powers to resolve a great many raw material problems. But without enough energy, we will be virtually helpless. Such a blunt statement requires illustration.

Copper is an important material for industrial society; there is a great deal of it in the earth's crust, thousands of times more than we are consuming annually.[5] But most of this copper is in low-grade ores — that is, in ores that contain small amounts of copper. One very large mine in the United States is now using ore that has 5.8 pounds of copper per ton of ore.[6] The high-grade ores that offered 50 to 100 pounds per ton have long since been used up. Once, indeed, there was pure copper on or near the surface of the earth; it was used to make spear points during the Bronze Age. Today, there is no question that we can get copper from the low-grade ores that are so common, but only if we have the energy to operate the large machines that can handle vast amounts of rock — to dig it out of the ground, transport it, crush it, process it into copper, and haul away the spent ore. As long as we have the energy, then copper supplies are virtually inexhaustible. But if we do not have energy, the low-grade resources would be almost as unreachable as they were to primitive man and could be worked only in very small amounts. The copper in junkyards, old cars, and disused buildings would be better sources. None would be wasted; we would handle copper the way we presently handle more valuable metals. No conservation organization has to call for recycling gold since its economic value does that automatically.

For most minerals, current domestic production comes largely from these relatively common low-grade ores. Whether this country is self-sufficient in minerals, then, is not so much a question of absolute scarcity as it is of the relative quality of our resources compared to foreign resources. When alarming figures are reported about our dependence on imported materials, it does not mean we are running out of resources. What it means is that foreign countries have higher grade ores that can be produced at a lower cost than our lower grade domestic resources. These imports are important to us because of their effect on our export-import balance, on the profitability of domestic producers, on the jobs they provide, and on our military security. They are not important indicators of whether or not we are running out of resources. In most cases we have the resources, and we could pass a law requiring the use of our own supplies. This would be a big boost to domestic producers; but for the consuming public, however, it will mean higher prices. For the country as a whole, it will mean using more of our own energy and resources to obtain the materials we use. In the 1950s and 1960s, a policy was established to restrict oil imports; it was known as the "drain America first" policy.

Aluminum provides the clearest illustration of the preeminence of energy over mineral scarcity. Aluminum is the most common metallic element on the

earth, comprising fully 8 percent of the earth's crust.
But it is also a very energy-intensive metal to produce
from its ore, requiring large amounts of electricity.
Some aluminum is produced in remote areas with a
surplus of hydroelectric energy, such as Canada and
Norway, but most is produced in areas where there are
other competing uses for electricity. Since aluminum
is not as essential as other metals in industrial society,
its production could drop despite its abundance; the
electrical energy would be used for more essential purposes. Cement is another example; it is made from
very common materials — limestone and clay — but the
process requires high temperatures. Plastics are perhaps a better example yet. They are made directly
from hydrocarbon fuels in the petrochemical industry.

Ours is still an age of steel. Per capita consumption,
at 1,560 pounds per year, dwarfs the figure for its
nearest competitors: aluminum, at 35 pounds per
year, and copper, at 15 pounds per year. How available is steel then, and does it require the same costly
energy expenditures as copper and aluminum? Fortunately, not only is iron ore very common, comprising 5
percent of the earth's crust, but steel can be produced
from iron ore without the use of too much energy.
Coal, the essential fuel required, is the most common
fossil fuel, so it is safe to say that the prospects for steel
are good. This is fortunate since iron and steel are the
only nonrenewable materials that are absolutely essential for a world that would otherwise be able to get by
on renewable resources.

In sum, if energy is available, the prospects for most metals are good, at least for the foreseeable future. True, there are several question marks. Some of the alloying elements used to make specialized steels have very restricted sources. Cobalt, for example, which is necessary to make the alloy steel used in turbine blades that must be both light and able to withstand high speeds and temperatures, is primarily obtained as a byproduct of several copper mines in Zaire. Tungsten is used to make the special steels for machine tools that are sufficiently heat-resistant to cut other high-grade steels without softening. Most of it comes from China. And then there are several commonly used metals that do not seem to have the abundance of low-grade ores; lead and zinc are two examples.

The speed with which the outlook for specific materials can change is striking. There was some concern about sulfur reserves after World War II, but now we have a surplus because it is accumulating around the plants which remove it from high-sulfur oil. Platinum, once used primarily in jewelry, is now being used in catalytic mufflers to reduce the air pollution from cars, and it could become scarce quickly if this use continues. Removing lead from gasoline has eased the concern for its availability, and the price of mercury dropped precipitously when its use as a seed fungicide was banned. A great deal of helium will be needed in the future if superconductors of electricity go into service to improve the efficiency of electrical transmission. Helium is a byproduct of several natural gas fields in

Kansas and New Mexico, so its supply will dwindle as natural gas is depleted.

Such rapid changes make the job of assessing materials very difficult. But generally we should be able to get by without too much difficulty if energy is available to drive the powerful tools we have.

The story is much the same with agriculture. With plentiful energy, a world population several times larger than at present could be fed and fed well. Water could be desalinated or pumped wherever needed to make the deserts bloom. Chemical fertilizers could be produced to increase agricultural yields around the world. Increased food processing could reduce the spoilage that now occurs in many less developed countries. Transportation could be used to move foods from areas where expanded production is possible to areas where food is needed.

If the energy available to agriculture declined, however, agricultural production would inevitably fall, although how much is very hard to predict. Many unproductive, sandy soils can now be used because they take chemical fertilizers so well and are easy to work, but without the energy to produce the fertilizers, many such soils would not be worth the tilling. The areas irrigated with deep wells or pumped distribution systems would revert to dryland agriculture, and desert sites would cease production altogether. Today, a number of these areas are producing two or three crops a year. With less energy available for transportation or food processing, populations would begin to move to the food-producing areas. It would no longer be feasible to move the food to the consumers as we do today. But the most important factor would be the drop in yields everywhere if the use of chemical fertilizers dropped significantly. It takes energy to produce chemical fertilizers (as well as insecticides and herbicides). Nitrogen is especially sensitive to energy availability since so much of it is used It is made directly from fuels — primarily natural gas — rather than from mineral deposits, as is the case with phosphorous and potassium. It is already becoming more expensive, and if use declines, yields will no doubt decline also. Agricultural methods would then begin to change, and techniques from the past would have to be reintroduced to maintain soil fertility — techniques such as crop rotation, cover crops, fallowing, composting, and the use of manure. But even with these measures, yields would fall.

Contrary to popular belief, agricultural machines are not an important factor since they do not necessarily improve yields. Americans frequently have the mistaken notion that because we are the world's largest producer of food and have the most mechanized agriculture, we also produce the highest yields per acre. But this is not so. Small countries that are trying to reduce their food imports, such as Holland, Belgium, England, and Japan, manage to achieve significantly higher yields per acre than we do. For example, the *FAO Production Yearbook* for 1976 reports that U.S. wheat farms produce an average of 1,660 pounds of grain per acre. The figure for Holland is 5,107

per acre. U.S. rice yields average 4,434 pounds per
acre; Japan averages 5,200 pounds per acre; and
Spain averages 5,607 pounds per acre. Belgium and
England both produce over 100,000 pounds of toma-
toes per acre, three times our average. They achieve
these yields primarily by keeping farms small and by
putting more labor into agriculture than we do. Machinery is one agricultural use of energy that can be
cut down without reducing yields, distinguishing it
sharply from the energy that goes into fertilizers and irrigation. In other words, as energy becomes more
expensive, its use will be curtailed first in farm machinery.

A simple listing of the ways energy is used in agriculture does not really give the full picture, however. It is
also necessary to mention the ways energy is *not* used.
A great deal of land was released to produce crops
when fossil fuels replaced wood for household heating
and cooking, when tractors replaced draft animals,
and when trucks and cars replaced horse-drawn transportation. This meant that land formerly used for
woods or pastures could be put to raising crops for human consumption. Put another way, fossil fuels are in-
directly being turned into food. Thus, as fossil fuels decline, the impact on agriculture will be accentuated
and will go beyond the issue of energy scarcity. Land
will become more of an issue than it already is in this
overpopulated world.

Is the food situation hopeless then if fossil fuels run
out? The question is complicated by the radically dif-

ferent situation worldwide between the developed and the underdeveloped countries. (We will turn to the underdeveloped countries in a later chapter.) If we focus on the developed world, it is safe to say that no survival question is involved. We can make a number of adjustments to reduce our dependence on energy in agriculture. The most obvious one would be to reduce the animal products in our diet. We have to remember that our whole way of life is a reflection of abundance. Not only did we have vast grazing lands with no economic use except for grazing animals, but we also had grain surpluses which we chose to use by feeding to animals. Because of this, we developed a diet heavy in animal protein, and although we have come to feel that this diet is essential for good nutrition, there is now good evidence that other diets more frugal in their land requirements are healthier.[7] The peasants of Vilcamba Valley in Ecuador, where the chances of living to a hundred are three hundred times better than in the United States, are reported to have a diet of only 1,200 calories per day compared to 3,300 here; the peasants eat very little meat or dairy products.[8] And, consider China, which is roughly the same size as the United States but has less arable land and at least four times as many people. In recent times, it has managed to feed itself well on a diet that is largely grains and vegetables, with animal products used primarily for flavoring. How necessary animal proteins are in a diet depends more on the protein balance among all foods than on the amount of animal protein alone. With certain diets, it is possible to do without animal protein altogether.

With food, at least, it is safe to say that we have the resources as well as the flexibility to adjust to energy shortages. And what resource could be more important? We are the Arabs of agriculture, and, unlike the Arabs, our resource will last more than a few decades. Having an abundance of land, the vital resource, we are far better off than any other major country in the world. Even with the worst possible energy future, we have enough land to feed ourselves well and still have food for other peoples. Let us hope it causes us to be generous and conciliatory to others, rather than proud and arrogant.

If the future of minerals and agriculture productivity depends largely on the future of energy, what, then, are the prospects for energy? This is, unfortunately, a very complex question, dealing not only with the resources still in the ground and the technology to exploit them, but also the question of economics. What are the costs of energy from different sources? What quantities can be provided? How long will it take to develop new sources? Will the capital be available to finance them? On top of these questions are all the political questions: How much should energy cost? Who should benefit from the rise in price of energy resources still in the ground? And how can conservation be encouraged?

In the face of all these complexities, it can be called progress just to have reached the point where there is general agreement that there is an energy problem. The skepticism about the energy shortage has finally given way. It survived the Arab oil boycott since that event could logically be seen as a political move and not an expression of physical scarcity. Environmentalists too regularly reflected skepticism about the energy shortage when they opposed all large-scale energy developments — offshore drilling, the Alaskan pipeline, nuclear plants, strip mining, dams — with the assurance that "other" better sources of energy were available. Indeed, just a few years ago, geologists held widely divergent opinions about the remaining amounts of oil and gas. A recent energy textbook lists seventeen different estimates of domestic oil remaining to be discovered, and the amounts ranged from 50 to 466 billion barrels.[9] No wonder there was confusion.

But in 1977 when President Carter presented his energy program, there was virtual consensus about the seriousness of the picture painted, even though political disagreements remained over how to deal with it. The bitter cold of the previous winter had brought the natural gas shortage uncomfortably close to many homes, and on top of that, the CIA was reporting that world oil resources were not as large as previously expected. The most serious matter for us, however, was the decline in production of domestic oil and gas that had begun in the early 1970s, necessitating greatly increased oil imports that led to huge trade deficits and the weakening of the dollar. Of all the estimates of our remaining supplies of oil and gas, the most pessimistic one, by M. K. Hubbert, was turning out to be correct.[10] If his projections continue to be close to the mark, by the year 2000, oil and gas production will have fallen to one-third of the maximum production levels of the early 1970s.

If there is one key difference between the contemporary energy situations and the resource challenges that industrial society has surmounted in the past, it is the *scale* of our use of oil and gas today. We are using over six billion barrels of oil per year (at 42 gallons a barrel), a figure so large it is hard to comprehend. On a per capita basis, it comes to about *1,200 gallons per person per year*. Even more staggering, oil is only about 45 percent of our energy use; natural gas comprises another 28 percent. Alaskan north slope oil deposits are estimated to be between ten and twenty-five billion barrels; the higher figure would provide our oil needs for only four years if that source alone were used.

Thus, to replace oil and gas with some other form of energy would be a task of almost unbelievable proportions. Assuming that alternatives are available, consider the oil wells, pipelines, refineries, and distribution facilities that would have to be replaced with facilities that undoubtedly would be much more expensive. With all the construction of nuclear power plants that has gone on in recent years, nuclear energy still provided only 2.5 percent of our energy in 1976, or about the same as firewood!

The factor of scale is what makes the energy question so totally different from, say, the space program, another massive government program. It was possible to put unlimited resources into a few space vehicles, but such an effort cannot be expanded thousands of times to provide new energy supplies throughout the country without exceeding our productive capacity many times over. Construction work on the scale needed would itself require a large amount of energy, radically reducing the energy available to the rest of society.

Another factor of major importance is the *time* it would take to develop new sources on the scale required. Virtually all the technological developments on which our hopes are pinned — fusion, breeders, solar and wind projects, geothermal fields, coal gasification and liquefaction — require research and development time schedules that could drag out to the end of this century. It is a long process to develop an alternative source of energy. The theoretical work must be done and laboratory models designed and built, then scaled up into small prototypes to test different schemes. A commercial-sized prototype must be built based on the best scheme, which, if successful, must then be replicated around the country before a significant amount of energy is produced. The step of building and testing the full-sized prototype is especially time-consuming and can take ten to fifteen years in itself. All steps entail the design of new machinery and new construction processes, and the final product must be extensively tested and evaluated. So far, no large-scale alternative stacks up very well in the face of the questions of economic feasibility and environmental impact. Once President Carter had all the relevant information, he had very little choice in handling the energy shortage other than the policies he announced: conservation and the expansion of coal production, with oil imports making up the shortfall.

Coal! Who would have thought a few years ago that dirty, old-fashioned, polluting coal would be the wave of the future? It was supposed to have been the fuel of the nineteenth century, not the twenty-first. What happened to all those pollution-free, high-technology alternatives in shining new plants that were to carry industrial society into the future? As it turns out, they either cannot get off the ground, or they cannot compete with coal. Coal is the only source of energy with the practical assets that are necessary; it is available on the *scale* required, and the technology exists today to put it to use *quickly* with much less air pollution than in the past, and with strip-mined lands restored. In many ways it is miserable stuff, and it will not make us independent of foreign oil, but it is the best alternative we have at this time.

Because coal deposits lie in continuous seams that can be identified over large areas, there is no question that we have a lot of it. Whereas we have used some 60 percent of our oil and gas, only 5 percent of our coal has been used.[11] It can be put to use quickly, too, in electrical generating plants and in other industries where it can be substituted for oil and gas. It is already starting to go back into use in household heating, either to reduce fuel bills or as a back-up for natural gas in areas where supplies are particularly uncertain.

The big technological breakthrough that is being looked for, which, if achieved, will assure coal's dominance in the future, is to gasify and liquefy it. This synthetic oil and gas would have all sorts of advantages over solid coal: pollutants could be removed from the synthetic fuels that cannot be removed from solid coal; they could go into existing oil and gas distribution systems; and they could be used in ways solid coal cannot be used, such as in turbines, internal combustion engines, and as a feed stock for the petrochemical industry. So far, however, the research work on synthetic fuels from coal is going slowly. Although there is no question it can be done; there are questions about its cost, the amount of energy lost in the conversion, and whether the operation can be scaled up adequately to provide significant quantities of fuel.[12] At present, the best prospect seems to be to heat coal *in situ* (underground, without mining it), which drives off a gas with a low-energy content. But such gas cannot be economically transported by pipeline; users would have to come to the source. There is little chance of much synthetic fuel being available in this century, but it is a technology which, if successful, will have a marked bearing on the next century. In the meantime, advances, such as fluidized bed combustion and solvent-refined coal, hold promise for the efficient generation of electricity using coal.

Even though coal is our best prospect, its development will still take time. It takes time to open new mines, build coal slurry pipelines, and convert industries from oil and gas to coal. The problem, in fact, will be how to get coal into use rapidly enough to slow our rapidly growing dependence on imported oil. Coal will not be all that cheap either, with the requirements of the pollution-control devices and full restoration of strip mines. Unless the price of oil and gas is allowed to rise substantially or absolute scarcities are encountered, there will be little economic incentive to switch to coal, and new mines will not be opened.

Whether or not we like coal is almost beside the point. It is analogous to the Alaskan pipeline. We may have preferred to do without it, but if it is a matter of preserving jobs, providing at least some opportunities for the young people of the baby-boom generation who are now looking for jobs, and letting old people stay in their homes, we will do what has to be done. Coal will provide the competition that other forms of energy will have to meet if they are to see much use. So far, it looks as if coal is coming in well ahead of other alternatives.

At the moment, nuclear energy is the most serious contender, but its prospects for making more than a minor contribution to the energy picture seem to be diminishing steadily. It is worth spending some time on the subject because so many high hopes have been fostered by the nuclear industry.

The questions of plant safety and disposal of nuclear wastes that preoccupy us now are not the most fundamental problems with conventional nuclear energy;

they could go either way depending on how badly we want the modest amount of energy that nuclear power can provide. The uncontested fact is that uranium supplies for conventional reactors are limited.[13] Uranium is one of the rarest elements on earth, and conventional nuclear reactors utilize only a tiny fraction of it, the isotope U-235, which is 0.7 percent of naturally occurring uranium. Not surprisingly, it is becoming very expensive. On top of the limited fuel supplies, nuclear power plants are becoming extremely expensive to build, and their economic prospects have been further eroded by their poor record of reliability, especially the newer, larger ones. Safety requirements for nuclear power plants are complex and expensive, and malfunctions that can be tolerated in other power plants cause nuclear plants to be shut down. All indications are that coal-fired power plants have better economic prospects, as well as being safer, more reliable, and utilizing a fuel with far larger reserves.

Because existing reactors use uranium so inefficiently, the research thrust now is toward the breeder reactor because it can use the common isotope of uranium, U-238, which comprises 99.3 percent of naturally occurring uranium. The U-238 is used by "breeding" it into plutonium in a reactor specially designed for this purpose. With breeder reactors, the fuel problem would be resolved, but the questions of safety would become paramount since these reactors are so much more dangerous than conventional reactors. To breed uranium into plutonium requires a much higher

power density in the reactor core, which means that
the fuel must be concentrated into a smaller space. It
still cannot explode in a mushroom-shaped cloud, but
it is closer to that condition. Further, liquid sodium
must be used as a coolant because water cannot take
the heat away fast enough. This is dangerous because
sodium burns if it comes in contact with air or water,
so even simple leaks cannot be permitted. In addition,
there is the complication that plutonium itself is an extremely deadly material, and one which can easily be
made into atomic bombs.

The whole issue of breeder reactors has been aptly
termed a Faustian bargain. It is the best proof that we
are in danger of becoming energy "junkies," willing to
do anything to maintain our "habit." Fortunately, the
early indications are that breeder reactors will be
much more expensive than conventional reactors because of their greater complexity and safety requirements. Thanks to coal and to economics, we should
not have to be tempted to make the Faustian bargain.

Fusion is the third form of nuclear energy, and it requires special comment because it is the ideal one, the
one form that could provide an unending supply of
safe energy for industrial society. Fusion gets its name
from the "fusing" of small atoms into larger ones, the
process that goes on in the sun. For fusion to occur, the
temperature and pressure must be comparable to that
on the sun. The fuel is deuterium, an isotope of hydro-
gen, and it is abundant in seawater. Very little radioactive waste is produced in a fusion reactor, and there is

no possibility of a runaway chain reaction as there is in conventional and breeder reactors. The problem, in fact, is just the opposite — to keep the reaction going. To simulate the conditions of the sun here on earth requires, among other things, temperatures of 180 million degrees Fahrenheit and containment of the superheated fuel that would melt any physical containers; magnetic forces are used instead. Some progress is being made on test reactors, and the actual production of fusion energy in the laboratory is expected soon. But to scale this effort up to commercial proportions means that a number of major obstacles must be overcome. One of the most formidable problems is that no known material can withstand the high-energy particles that are generated in a fusion reactor; at its best it would destroy itself in a matter of several years. An assessment of the prospects of fusion energy in *Science,* the journal of the American Association for the Advancement of Science, concludes by saying, "It is sometimes necessary to suspend one's critical faculties to not find the problems of fusion overwhelming."[14]

It is possible that, with fusion energy, the advancement of technology may be reaching limits established by the nature of materials. But however it goes, fusion research deserves close scrutiny since it alone among the many high-technology alternatives holds out the prospect of a long life for industrial society.

If fusion energy has a dark side, it is the social and political consequences of this otherwise desirable technology. If fusion were successful, it would have a tendency to lead to greater centralization of power and increasingly strong government. Powerful technology requires powerful government to regulate it, just the opposite of smaller scale, more benign technology that is accessible to any craftsman and understandable by any city councilman. Some technologies are inherently totalitarian and nuclear energy is one of them.

There are, of course, many other sources of energy available. Some have greater potential than all fossil fuels put together, as their promoters never cease to point out. What they fail to mention is the difficulty of collecting energy from these sources and putting it to use. Some schemes consume so much energy that there is little net gain in energy in the process. The solar space station is the classic example; it will be feasible only if the energy cost of producing photovoltaic cells and getting them into space can be reduced significantly. Many energy sources are too "thin" to be collected efficiently, such as the temperature gradients of the ocean, the energy in waves, and the small amount of oil in a ton of oil shale; only if *in situ* processing (underground without mining) of oil shales can be accomplished will they produce much oil.[15] Some energy sources take so much costly hardware that they will never be able to compete with coal; large-scale solar and wind projects fall into this category, as do breeders. In many cases, development is going much slower than expected; very few dry steam geothermal fields have been found, the ideal kind, and the hot water fields frequently contain dissolved materials that damage heat exchangers. Some resources are just too small to be of much use; the remaining hydroelectric sites are either poor or their reservoirs would flood valuable agricultural or recreational land; tidal power has a fraction of the potential of hydroelectric; and garbage and manure will disappear as an energy resource as scarcity reduces the amount of waste generated. Some schemes seem to be blind efforts to maintain industrial society against all logic; energy farms have been proposed to produce wood wheat, water hyacinths, and algae, which would then be distilled into different forms of alcohol, almost surely with a net loss of energy or a modest gain at best. It just does not seem to occur to the originators of these schemes that it would make far more sense to burn the wood or eat the farm crops directly, without all the expensive hardware and handling necessary to convert them into industrial products, a point now being argued by scientists.[16]

The reality of most high-technology alternatives, then, is that more and more they are appearing to be poor investments, in dollar terms, in energy terms, or both. But they all should be pursued, just so we know what we have and what we do not have to face the future with. And while a breakthrough is possible at any time, there is no point in thinking about this possibility without also remembering that a setback is also possible — some unforeseen effect of modern technology on the atmosphere, the weather, or the public health. If the concern about carbon dioxide in the atmosphere turns out to be correct, for example, and the burning of fossil fuels had to be cut down, it is hard to imagine how it could be accomplished without bringing down industrial society in the process.

To sum up this large subject of the interplay of technology and natural resources, it seems safe to say that energy is clearly the limiting factor, at least as far as can be discerned at this time. The development of many alternative sources of energy are not working out as well as expected, but we do have coal resources which will buffer us from a catastrophic energy shortage as oil and gas are depleted. Coal, however, is unlikely to be available on the scale of oil and gas today, and, in a synthetic liquid or gaseous form, it is likely to be quite expensive. Even though we have a great deal of coal, it, too, is a nonrenewable resource. Today we are using the highest grade coals and those easiest to mine. In the long run, coal, too, will grow expensive and then fail.

There are other technologies that are failing already. Before we turn to the technologies that are likely to be winners in the future it is instructive to look at the losers.

Failing Technologies

Technology can fail in a number of ways; foremost among them is cost. Only rarely does the underlying scientific knowledge elude us. More commonly, scientific knowledge cannot be translated into practical devices that are economically feasible. This does not mean that we will have to pay more for something we need; the absence of economic feasibility means that its cost will be more than it is worth; it will not be bought or used. Similarly, if a machine requires so much energy to operate that the value of the work it does falls behind the cost to operate the machine, the machine will be abandoned. It is energy that has made modern technology so powerful; without energy, it would be useless. As energy gets scarce and the price is forced up, much of our technology will become progressively less useful to us.

Only if the prospects for energy can be reversed and its cost brought down is technology likely to play the dominant role in social change that it has in the recent past. Then there was no stopping it, expecially when technological advance was teamed up with abundant resources and the free enterprise system; profit was the perfect motivation to bring new technology into use. But this era is passing. New technology has now become so complex and expensive that even the largest corporations shy away from the cost of developing it, especially when the chances for success are dim. The government is left with the task of developing new forms of transportation, new energy sources, and cures for the diseases of affluence — cancer, heart disease, diabetes, and others.

The SST was the first shiny new technology to fail. The United States had the foresight to see this in 1971, and the Anglo-French Concorde is now proving that the decision was correct. Many remain unsold, production has stopped, and existing service is largely a face-saving effort, and an expensive one at that. The sonic boom restricts the SST to oceanic routes, and even at subsonic speed it is noisy. But such environmental problems can be lived with if people choose, although there have been disturbing reports of damage to the ozone layer that protects us from ultraviolet radiation. The more immediate barrier to the SST is that any time speed is doubled, the wind resistance increases eight times, and fuel consumption skyrockets. Only if there were a superabundance of energy could the exponential increases in travel speeds we have experienced in the past be continued into the future. Just a decade ago, the SST was seen as the inevitable next step that air travelers could look forward to. Now, all of a sudden, it looks absurd, all that noise and energy simply to get business people across the Atlantic a few hours faster. What could they do with those hours saved that could be worth the costs and the environmental insults?

The shift in our thinking about the SST is part of a much broader change. We no longer can base predictions on the trend lines that have gone up and up for such a long time. The projections of increasing travel speeds led past the SST to space travel, and the successes of the space program were right on track with the expectations of generations of science fiction writers. Space travel does have the asset of being frictionless, yet it requires massive amounts of energy to escape the gravitational pull of the earth or any other heavenly bodies visited. In science fiction, the space vehicles always had some unnamed but highly concentrated fuel supply that enabled them to move about with impunity. No such energy source is on the horizon; our rockets are primarily just huge fuel tanks. The manned vehicles are already being replaced by smaller unmanned ones, and unless some new energy source is developed, space exploration will soon be restricted to radio waves and other electronic means.

Those looking forward to a space age Renaissance will view our restriction to earth as a form of imprisonment, stunting the imagination and frustrating our pioneer spirit. Perhaps we need to realize that the pioneer spirit can lead to a form of escapism, a way of running away from problems. As it becomes clear that we will not be able to export our surplus population to other planets or shoot our radioactive wastes into space, the long youth of technological man will come to an end. Just thinking again of the beautiful little planet we live on will be a step toward maturity.

High-speed ground transportation is the next technology that can be expected to fail. We hear much about Japan's "bullet" train, but the noise it makes is horrendous for the large number of people living along its route, and vibrations from it have caused buildings to crack. Its energy consumption is high because of wind resistance. A train that goes half as fast, say a reasonable sixty miles an hour, is far less noisy, and the passengers can enjoy the view of the passing scene.

Rapid transit is already failing, not so much because

of the energy requirements, but because of the impossible construction job it would require to serve our sprawling cities adequately. If riders were to walk no more than a half a mile to a rapid transit station — a reasonable distance if people are to be diverted from their cars — it would be necessary to build thousands of miles of lines and hundreds of stations to serve a major city. The cost is staggering, as many cities have discovered after planning very limited systems. Buses are more likely to be the "wave of the future" in urban transportation, retrieved from the same oblivion that coal was heading for. They are inexpensive to purchase; they can use existing roadways without new construction, and service can be expanded incrementally as people are forced from their cars by the energy shortage.

When I was young, people were intrigued by the prospect of flying around in their own personal helicopters. It seemed logical enough then. Now we will be lucky if we have our cars for another generation or two. The final stage of the progression will be when people get around by walking or bicycling in the small towns or small cities that are likely to become more popular as energy becomes scarce. Hopefully, such new urban arrangements will be as pleasant as many cities and towns were in the past, with their intimacy and liveliness and the countryside a short distance away.

Urban renewal has already failed, and the office towers, the huge apartment blocks, and the regional shopping centers are likely to follow as energy gets scarcer. Urban renewal projects are the kind of grandiose designs that can be built only with a surplus of energy and a concentration of economic power. In the past, similar monuments were built by totalitarian regimes that could organize enough slaves to build the Pyramids, or a "proper" capital for an empire, or to exploit enough peasants to create a Versailles. Our megastructures will at least provide a vast storehouse of steel, aluminum, glass, and copper for future use.

One piece of advanced engineering that will never have the opportunity for success before failing is the prototype waste-recovery plant recently built near San Diego. It was designed to recycle two hundred tons of garbage a day. When viewed from a distance, the plant has all the appearances of an oil refinery, with towers and masses of pipes and conduits. On closer inspection it can be seen to be a maze of conveyer belts, choppers, screens, air separators, and literally hundreds of motors, pumps, and automatic valves — all used to separate the organic waste, glass, steel, and aluminum. Beyond that is the pyrolysis unit, the key element of the plant that is supposed to turn the organic material into a heavy oil. Completed for over a year, the plant still has not been able to operate for a full seventy-two-hour test run! Human hands could do the job better, but why bother? I look forward to the day when the job does not even need to be done, when all goods come in standardized glass containers, so that the contents can be seen and the containers returned for a deposit or kept at home for canning or other uses. When things are done in a reasonable way, the technological hurdles disappear.

There are several technologies that are failing because of indiscriminate use. For example, the routine use of insecticides is a perfect way to develop insects that are resistant to insecticides, since only the insects that are not killed by the sprays survive to reproduce. More ominously, indiscriminate use of antibiotics is producing disease organisms that are resistant to antibiotics. Excessive use of genetically uniform grains has led to the rapid evolution of plant diseases that thrive on them.

While technology undoubtedly is still expanding the niche of industrial society by turning valueless stuff into useful resources, it is losing some battles, too, some major ones. In addition, we are consuming part of the niche every day when we deplete nonrenewable resources, or when the genetic pool is reduced, or when the productivity of land is permanently diminished. And now it looks as if we may not be able to utilize parts of the niche that we know exist, such as low-grade ores and marginal energy sources.

But the technologies we are presently using are not the only ones available. A gentle technology of proven effectiveness already exists, drawn from the past as well as the present. If technology is to be integrated with the conservation of resources, it will be this gentle kind, a simple, frugal technology, that we must turn to sooner or later.

Winning Technologies

Through most of human history, people have relied on renewable resources — sun, wind, water, land. They got by well enough, and so could we. But consider the advantages we can employ to improve on their material existence. Even if all our worst fears about the disappearance of nonrenewable resources were realized over the next several hundred years, life could be comfortable.

We would have solar heating to avoid the cold and dampness that in the past sickened children and stiffened the bones of old people in winter. Solar-heated hot water would mean the comfort of hot baths and general cleanliness. Today solar energy is expensive because consumers demand constant availability at the touch of a switch. But when these requirements are relaxed, solar energy will be provided inexpensively. There are many alternatives to the costly collectors, storage tanks, pumps, and controls. Black tanks placed on the roofs can produce hot water very inexpensively for late afternoon bathing. Greenhouses built on the south side of houses can heat homes in the daytime; and water-filled metal tanks in the greenhouses can provide heat storage for nighttime and cloudy periods. Masonry walls inside glass walls can efficiently store heat that can be radiated into the home at night. Windows and eaves can be placed so as to collect solar energy in the winter but be shaded in the summer; and deciduous trees can be used to much the same effect. A small, well-insulated home can be maintained comfortably with very modest amounts of energy other than solar.

Wind can be used for a number of mechanical tasks that can wait to be done whenever the wind blows, such as pumping water. But its greatest usefulness will be to generate the modest amounts of electricity — to be stored in batteries — needed for lights, radios, and many small appliances and tools. (It is important to keep in mind that solar energy and wind energy require the materials and products of advanced technology, such as glass, plastics, and copper. If industrial technology should be disrupted by civil strife or for any other reason, life would become a much tougher proposition for the survivors.)

Methane gas is another source of energy. It can be used for cooking, lighting, refrigeration, and other purposes. Methane is produced when organic matter is allowed to decompose in the absence of air. The energy content of the waste is released as methane, the main component of natural gas, rather than as heat, as in compost piles where air is present. Anything organic can be put into a methane digester — newspapers, grass clippings, manure, or human wastes — but the process is most useful in areas where organic materials are easily available and where wastes are less apt to have the chemicals that poison the bacteria that produce the methane. The ideal thing about methane digesters is that after the gas is removed from the digester, the remaining slurry is an excellent fertilizer.

The whole process is one of those truly beautiful ones in which the waste is fully utilized for its energy and material content. As such, it is superior to composting and all other waste disposal methods in which the energy, materials, or both are lost

Some form of back-up energy will be necessary to supplement these renewable resources. In many cases this will be firewood, which has more potential than is generally realized. The energy content of wood is about that of coal, on the average, and there is a great deal of land that has limited economic usefulness except to grow trees. Firewood can be considered a way to collect and store the solar energy that falls on such land. And because the energy in wood is relatively concentrated, it can be transported considerable distances and still leave a substantial net gain in energy. Further, certain trees can have their limbs cut back to the trunk and grow new ones the following year. The trees that line so many country lanes in Europe were at one time harvested each year for wood supplies this way, a process known as pollarding.

A number of renewable resources can be used in cities as they exist today with substantial savings in fossil fuels. Although some of the more elaborate techniques are not economical today, they will become feasible when the price of oil and gas goes up. The greatest independence from a struggling industrial system will only be possible closer to the most important renewable resource of all, land. Capturing solar energy in agricultural crops or woods is more efficient than many sophisticated energy alternatives now being explored, but land is still essential to this use of solar energy.

The relative importance of agricultural land in the future may be the best indicator of how smoothly the transition from an economy of affluence to an economy of frugality is going. Land is the most conservative of all resources since it is the only one that can turn solar energy directly into food and fuel. In the future, if the price of land goes substantially above the value suggested by its economic return, it will be an indication of a lack of confidence in the social processes in this country and a signal of changing values. We will know that industrial society is failing when sons obey their fathers in order to remain in good standing for an inheritance of land, and when a daughter's marriage is evaluated according to whether or not a perspective groom has enough land to support her. Such extremes need never occur if the adaptation to scarcity is smooth and efficient, since many other economic activities should exist besides those directly associated with land.

But one thing, at least, we can be assured of: the necessary technology to live comfortably on renewable resources exists. It is simple and within the reach of everyone. It involves none of the desperate seeking after technological breakthroughs that characterize our present concerns for the future of urban industrial society. And these sustainable technologies will inexorably be brought into use by economic changes now under way.

CHAPTER IV

The Subsidence

The increase in raw material prices since 1972 is a change of far-reaching significance. It is not just another price increase. More than any other single indicator, higher prices for raw materials point to the onset of a new era, the era of scarcity.

Ever since the first achievements of the Industrial Revolution, there has been a downward trend in the prices of raw materials. Even recently, between 1950 and 1971, the government's index of *Crude Materials for Further Processing,* a component of the wholesale price index, fell 39 percent after corrections for inflation. The materials included in this index — foodstuffs, fuels, and materials for manufacturing and construction — dropped in price in real terms. This was primarily because machinery was introduced that displaced labor. The farmers, miners, and loggers that were displaced by machines had to find other work, and the jobs that were available were in the plants that were producing the cars, refrigerators, televisions, and other consumer goods. *These goods could not have*

*been produced before when so much labor was tied up
in agriculture and other raw material industries.* The
gross national product went up, and as long as material prices kept falling, it was inevitable that incomes
would increase. Between the same years of 1950 and
1971, per capita disposable income rose 56 percent,
again after corrections for inflation. Those were the
"good old days" — the niche of industrial society still
had room for expansion.

Figure 1 shows the two indexes — incomes and raw
material prices — moving steadily in opposite directions until 1971. But at this point, the pattern changes.
Raw material prices increased abruptly during 1972-
1974, a time of a booming economy worldwide. Demand for a number of commodities exceeded supplies
and pushed prices up, and on top of this, OPEC — the
Organization of Petroleum Exporting Countries —
added its price increases for oil. The recession that followed the 1972-1974 boom brought prices back somewhat; many scarcities, like those of copper and sugar,
"disappeared" as the recession dampened demand.
Since then, prices have risen, but much more slowly
and erratically. Even so, the substantial jump in the
real prices of raw materials since 1971 means that the
niche of industrial society is beginning to fill up and
materials are becoming scarcer. Higher prices are a
distinct signal of this effect.

Under normal circumstances, as raw material prices
rise, incomes fall, just the reverse of the process that
went on until 1971. Since 1971, higher prices should

have led to a broad-based effort to develop new raw material sources — especially energy — and to improve the efficiency of using existing supplies. Such efforts would inevitably take labor and capital away from other uses, leaving us with less consumer goods and services. To a degree, this has occurred. New energy resources in Alaska and on the continental shelf are being developed, resources that are significantly more expensive to exploit than the resources close to home that we used in the past. Also, a great deal more money is being "exported" to the oil-producing countries to pay for the rapidly increasing amounts of oil we import from them, money that formerly stayed in this country to buy goods for us. Both of these changes have taken income from the American worker. But somehow, against economic logic, we have managed to keep incomes rising rapidly along with raw material prices; only in 1974 did a high rate of inflation cause incomes to fall behind raw material prices.

How can real incomes continue to rise as raw material prices increase? It is a complicated question, and there are other factors involved besides natural resources, but it appears that incomes have been maintained by two devices. One is the very large federal deficits that have been carried each year since 1974. Between 1974 and 1977, the deficits averaged $61.5 billion annually, a huge amount of money to be pumped into the economy each year. Federal taxes were $287 less per person each year than would have been neces-

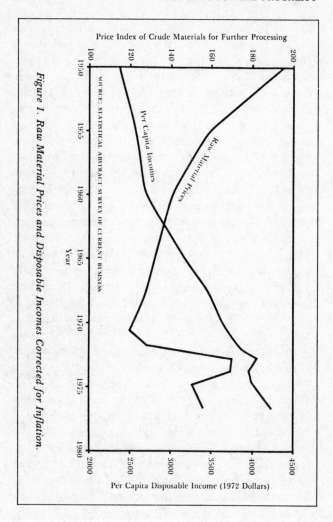

Figure 1. Raw Material Prices and Disposable Incomes Corrected for Inflation.

sary to balance the budget. For a typical family of four, this provided almost $1,200 of extra income a year! Secondly, there has been broad resistance to incomes falling behind the cost of living. In response to higher costs of living, the tendency is to push wages up along with prices, to maintain purchasing power. One of the consequences has been to discourage employment because of the high cost of employing people. In short, incomes are being maintained at unrealistically high levels by the federal deficits and by the general rigidity to falling wages. *We are paying ourselves too much.* The burden of resource scarcity is being shifted to future taxpayers and the unemployed.

In one respect, the cost of our excesses is being paid by all of us as the dollar falls in value. This is an indication of international loss of faith in a country that is living beyond its means. Imported goods and foreign travel become more expensive; but more important, if OPEC should raise oil prices to recover what it has lost because of the fall in the dollar, it would mean another huge increase in the cost of imported oil.

Not only should our incomes be lower than they are, but raw material prices should be higher. We have been shielded from higher prices by the price controls on oil and natural gas that have had strong public support in Congress. We have done this to keep fuel prices down and to preserve jobs. Domestic oil and natural gas prices have been held well below world prices that more truly reflect the scarcity of energy. Economists sometimes argue that OPEC oil prices are unrealistic

in relation to the cost of production. This is certainly
true; it costs only a few cents to pump a barrel of oil
from the rich oil deposits of the Persian Gulf area. But
to base prices only on the cost of production would
mean that the oil itself has no value, which is clearly
not the case. The last oil pumped from these fields
some fifty years from now will certainly have a far
higher value than the first oil pumped out during the
era of oil surpluses. The heavy demand for oil now and
the limited number of sources — which is a measure of
scarcity — have enabled OPEC to sustain their price increases without difficulty.

In this country, any suggestion that domestic oil
prices be allowed to rise to world levels is resisted because it would give windfall profits to the oil companies, and also because it would increase the cost of
living and threaten jobs. But with prices held low, the
use of energy has continued to increase, and, since our
domestic oil production is falling, the only way to provide enough oil is through increased imports. Elsewhere, in Europe, Japan, and the less developed countries, the only alternative has been strict conservation.
Use of energy in Europe at the start of 1977 was 14 percent below what it would have been if earlier growth
rates had continued.[1] Only in this country are we able
to maintain for a while longer our make-believe world
in which energy is still abundant.

In 1971, imports accounted for 15 percent of our oil;
by 1977, the figure was 43 percent. It is unlikely that
OPEC will allow us to purchase a continually increas-

ing amount of oil in the future, simply because to do so would deplete their resources too rapidly. Sooner or later, OPEC will either increase the price of oil to discourage our extravagant use, or simply place a limit on the amount we can buy. Before that happens, however, it may be that revenues from our exports will fall far enough behind the spiraling cost of imported oil to cause the value of the dollar to deteriorate to the point that we will not be able to finance a continued high level of imports. This is especially likely if other countries do not have the money to purchase our exports of food or manufactured goods.

Whatever the reason — a limit on OPEC exports, a balance of payment problem, or some unforeseen interruption of trade — when a real energy shortage occurs we will have to take real measures to cope with it — to reduce use and to further develop our own resources. At that time, there is no question that we will have to pay the full world market price of the energy we use. We will have to reallocate labor and capital to the task of adjusting to less energy consumption, taking them from other sectors of the economy. Industries that are currently using large amounts of energy will be squeezed, especially if they are producing luxuries rather than essentials. The laborers released by such a squeeze will hopefully find jobs either improving the efficiency with which we use the energy we have, or producing energy from sources that are currently uneconomical.

When such a reallocation of productive capacity occurs, it will inevitably mean that consumption of consumer goods will drop and that real incomes will fall. There is no way to take labor and energy from the consumer sector of the economy without reducing the production and consumption of goods. Not just individuals, but corporations will also feel the bite. In the reallocation of productive resources, some industries will gain — primarily those that either produce raw materials and energy or use it sparingly — but most will lose as the era of economic growth ends and the subsidence begins.

The Relative Price of
Raw Materials and Labor

It is the *relative price* of raw materials compared to that of labor that is the key variable in trying to understand how the subsidence will occur. Until now, labor has been the expensive commodity; energy and machinery were inexpensive and were used to save labor. Manufacturers will always try to use the cheapest inputs to conserve the costly ones, and, characteristically, this has meant using machines to save labor. Up until recently, the successful firms were the ones that had the capital to build the automated plants that used the least labor. In the future, as the relative costs of labor and materials change, labor will become a better buy than it is today. Wages need not actually fall for this to happen; it is more likely that materials and equipment will inflate in price much more rapidly than wages, and *real income* will fall, to use the economists' term. But whichever way it goes, machines and energy will become more expensive, and an entirely different set of characteristics will emerge in our economy. Labor will begin to replace machines. The effect of this change on the conservation of resources will be dramatic.

The early warning signals are already visible. Energy-intensive industries are starting to feel the pinch. The auto industry would be happy to get back to the peak year of 1973, when 9.6 million domestic cars were sold. Prices for new homes are rapidly going beyond the reach of the majority of Americans, causing more and more old homes to be restored; the cheap materials for new housing that permitted old dwellings to be torn down in the past are no longer available. Similarly, the repair business is gaining as people avoid purchasing expensive new items by fixing up what they have. Many airlines are not profitable enough to replace their aircraft, and the aircraft manufacturers presently make most of their income on government-funded military and space programs.

As time passes and incomes begin to fall, many shifts to labor from machines will occur. Machines that have the most marginal economic productivity will be the first to go. A large piece of construction equipment will not be brought in to do a task several men can do by hand in a few hours. Small neighborhood grocery stores will begin to reappear as the cost to drive the family car to the supermarket goes up. In agriculture, instead of spraying entire fields routinely with a large machine or aircraft, a hand sprayer will be used to treat only the infected parts of a field. The efforts to develop large mechanical harvesters of fruits and vegetables that agricultural engineers have been working on with limited success for years will cease. Small-scale agriculture that uses labor instead of expensive equipment and chemicals will be more and more economical. The coal deposits that are common in many parts of this country will start to be worked by small-scale operations to serve local needs. Woodcutters will reappear in areas with timber unsuitable for lumbering.

A recent study has reported a significant new phenomenon: labor-intensive industries are now more profitable than capital-intensive ones.[2] In part this may reflect the profitability of the service industries, but it also reflects the squeeze being placed on manufacturing industries by increasing raw material prices. It is surprising to see this trend emerging so soon, but it is clearly a trend in line with a more frugal economy. Economists have already adjusted downward their estimates of future GNP growth due to energy constraints.[3]

Transportation is the single greatest consumer of energy. When all the energy costs of transportation are added together — for building and maintaining roads, for manufacturing vehicles and service facilities, and for the fuel used by the vehicles themselves — transportation accounts for 42 percent of all energy used in this country.[4] A rising price trend for energy will undoubtedly have a major effect on the geographical distribution of industry because of higher transportation costs, and this will reduce the scale of industrial plants. Energy scarcity will be the major force that brings about a goal long sought by many people: economic decentralization.

In the past, industrial operations became larger and larger as the falling costs of transportation enabled manufacturers to capitalize on the economies of scale offered by modern industrial processes. The savings accrued by large, efficient plants easily covered the additional transportation costs. This favored the rise of large corporations that had the capital to build huge plants and the distribution systems to get the vast production to nationwide and worldwide markets. With the advantage of cheap transportation and the savings from reduced labor requirements, the large manufacturing corporations were able to put a good part of their small competitors out of business.

But it is simply because these corporations were so well-suited to the past that they are likely to have problems in the future — and ultimately to fail. Using machines, energy, raw materials, and transportation extensively, they will find that they are using all the wrong inputs, all those that will be increasingly expensive in the future, but not the relatively inexpensive input — labor. Just as important, their specialized, automated plants will provide little flexibility to adapt to changing conditions. Instead, as demand for their products sag, they will have to increase prices in order to cover fixed costs and to pay the interest on borrowed capital.

On the other hand, decentralized, regional firms will find themselves in an improving situation as they begin to undersell their corporate competitors. Located close to their customers, they will not be so affected by rising transportation costs. Using less sophisticated machinery, they will have much more flexibility to modify both their products and their inputs in response to changing markets. Not only is equipment expensive these days and likely to become more so, but with capital scarce, interest rates are high, magnifying further the cost of modern plants. Most economists foresee an increasing scarcity of capital and higher interest rates.[5] The way to avoid these costs is with the use of labor, the input that will be increasingly available at a reasonable cost and which decentralized firms will be in a position to take advantage of. One can imagine new firms reoccupying unused or derelict buildings and employing makeshift equipment to avoid the high costs of a new plant and sophisticated equipment.

Because of the large amounts of capital required for modern plants, large firms could go bankrupt very quickly if their output declines enough to make the servicing of their debts impossible. In the face of declining sales, there is little doubt that these firms will try to utilize the plants they have as long as possible, but this effort will only give the new generation of regional manufacturing firms a chance to gain an advantage that declining national corporations may not be able to challenge. The vast sources of capital that have been available to large corporations will dry up very quickly when it appears that the big firms will not be as profitable in the future as they have been in the past. They may then find it very hard to obtain the capital to compete effectively with decentralized firms.

I realize how hard it is to imagine the demise of any large corporation. It must have been almost as hard a hundred years ago to imagine that the all-powerful railroads would be the economic cripples they are today. But the large, automated plants designed to serve a huge market are likely to end up as silent as most railroad stations are today, isolated by high transportation costs, energy-intensive processes, and inflexibility.

The Urban Impact

The same forces that threaten large national corporations also threaten our largest cities. In the past, the bigger a city the better its prospects were. With more size it could offer better transportation facilities, a larger work force with more skills, more of the specialized services necessary for modern economic activities, plus a record of economic success and growth — advantages that smaller cities could rarely match. In the last several decades, however, the first disadvantages of urban scale began to be felt — congestion, environmental deterioration, high crime rates, and high taxes. In the future, declining economic logic will be added to those. Large cities require more energy for their metabolism than smaller cities and towns, more energy to move people about, more energy to bring in goods and to export manufactured foods, and more energy to process wastes.

The cost of living and of doing business in large urban areas will go up with increases in the cost of energy, and there is not too much that can be done to adjust that situation. As with large manufacturing corporations, cities that have been the most prosperous in the postwar era will be least able to weather higher energy prices since they more clearly reflect the era of raw material abundance. They have the sprawling characteristic of the automobile era with extensive suburban development, rather than the compactness of the streetcar era. They are usually built around the interstate highway system rather than railroads or waterways, and they have the modern factories and the sleek office towers that are such heavy users of energy. Los Angeles is the classic example, but even older cities have suburban fringes. There are a few easy adjustments to be made; the inner cities can be recolonized to reduce transportation from suburbs; townhouses and apartments can be clustered around jobs and shopping centers; and public transportation can be expanded. But while such energy cost-cutting is possible and can help, it can only go so far. And it will not help the declining economic base of large cities compared to more decentralized, regional centers.

Jobs in the service industries and with government, so important in many large cities, may buffer cities somewhat. But many services, such as retailing, whole-saling, marketing, and financial services, are based on the flow of manufactured goods. All of these would de-cline if manufacturing declined or decentralized to a regional rather than a national base. Jobs with govern-ment could decline also if tax revenues fell along with economic output. As jobs in the large cities grow scarcer and the cost of living goes up, a low-paying job in a provincial city will start to look attractive, espe-cially if its long-term economic prospects are promis-ing and living costs are lower.

Pollution of all types should decline as the consump-tion of resources in our economy declines and the population begins to decentralize. The $500 billion price tag the Brookings Institution has placed on meet-ing the 1970 air pollution legislation and the 1972 water quality legislation would decrease.[6] We will no longer be able to afford a throwaway economy, litter-ing our cities and countryside with waste. The former pattern of truck farms around towns and cities will reappear, not only to absorb a city's organic waste and turn it into vegetables and fruits, but also to avoid the high cost of processed and fresh food that must be transported over long distances.

One of the most attractive aspects of increased re-gionalization will be the reemergence of regional dif-ferences out of the dulling sameness of so many places in this country today. The vast areas of single-crop agriculture will diversify to provide for local needs. Regional foods will emphasize the crops that thrive in the area. Building styles will reflect building materials available nearby and the local weather. The one-industry town should decline, along with its particular brand of instability and pollution. Conceivably, regional styles of clothing, music, dancing, and other cultural variables will reemerge with reduced mobility.

Part of the Jeffersonian ideal of rural life has always been that people be independent and self-sufficient. Higher prices for food and raw materials will provide more economic logic for such a way of life than today. Presently it is more a romantic image than a practical alternative. Jobs will start to appear in rural areas, in small towns, and in regional cities if — and this is the rub — wages are low enough relative to machinery, transportation, and energy to let small-scale, labor-intensive economic enterprises operate at a profit.

Why Personal Incomes Will Fall

The most unpleasant part of the process of adjusting to scarcity will undoubtedly be that people will be forced to make changes against their will as their incomes lag behind the cost of living — as real incomes fall. To many, it is incomprehensible that the government would allow real incomes to fall, corporate profits to decline, or the economic base of cities to erode. The issue invariably becomes what the government should do if such a situation threatens. More basically the question is: how should incomes and prices be determined? The only alternatives are the market and the political process.

The free market system has traditionally played the dominant role in our national ideology. Jefferson's dictum that "the best government is the least government" struck a very responsive chord in a frontier society bent on taking advantage of the resources that were abundantly available. Jefferson did not mean his statement as an endorsement of the free market system, but that was its effect. The government was rarely allowed to stand in the way of the free exploitation of resources and the God-given right to make money. Recently, however, capitalism and the free market have come in for some rough times, probably because in our mature industrial economy the market seems to reflect oppressive economic forces, dominated by powerful business and financial interests rather than individual opportunity as in the past. Yet at the same time, the antagonism to government and its meddlings has grown just as fast as the antagonism to the market. It seems that neither government nor the free market is able to release us from our torments or to return us to the way it was in the past before the niche of industrial society began to close in on us.

Price controls on oil and natural gas provide a good illustration of the frustrating business of using the government to hold the line against price increases generated by today's kind of market. Because oil and natural gas can be produced at a fraction of what they

118 MUDDLING TOWARD FRUGALITY

can be sold for, the argument goes, why should producers be allowed to make windfall profits on something that is so essential for everyone's livelihood? Price
controls were the obvious solution, and they worked for
a while. But anything that is underpriced will be used
to excess; if beef was twenty-five cents a pound, we
would eat more of it than we do (but cattlemen would
stop producing it). We have used more oil almost every
year, and at the same time, price controls have discouraged investment in expensive new energy sources
and energy-conservation devices, compounding the
shortages. The oil companies were handy scapegoats.
Their gains were justification for doing what we
wanted to do anyway — keep prices down and go on
consuming oil as if scarcity did not exist. It would have
been easy enough to decontrol prices and to place an
excess profits tax on the windfall profits of oil producers, or require that such profits be reinvested in alternative energy sources to reduce dependence on
imports. But price controls had broad political support, and the unpopular job of opposing them fell to
industry. Most congressmen, listening to the voters
back home, heard a consensus clearly opposed to higher prices. It was not until the value of the dollar fell so
much in 1978 that the energy bill presented to Congress contained some price increases.

The possibility of higher energy prices invariably
calls forth a widespread concern for the poor who cannot afford to pay the higher prices. Again, there is a
very efficient device for dealing with this problem — a

tax on energy that would be rebated on a per capita basis. The consumption of energy is, not surprisingly, closely related to income; the affluent consume much more than the poor,[7] and so the affluent would pay more into the tax fund than they received back, while the poor would receive more back than they paid in. But when a proposal for a rebated tax on gasoline was first made in 1974, it was rejected out of hand, and subsequent efforts by President Carter have faced stiff opposition.

Actually, one would have to be skeptical of the concern expressed for the poor when the general attitude toward welfare recipients in this country is so hostile. Welfare recipients are, after all, the poor of this country, but they are widely regarded simply as lazy or as welfare cheaters. This discrepancy in our concerns for the poor seems to suggest that our real concern is to avoid price increases for ourselves. That is entirely understandable, but it would be better to be honest about it.

The vast amount of energy being consumed in this country is being consumed primarily by the large middle class and the upper class, and that is where the major reduction in use must come from. Higher prices or higher taxes will do the job more efficiently than any other device. The federal-mandated mileage requirements for new cars will help, as will other regulatory efforts, but they cannot have nearly the pervasive effect on consumption that high prices would have. Higher prices would force customers to think about conserving energy at all times just to save money. We could, of course, sit tight and let market forces push prices up, but a rebated tax could encourage the same conservation much sooner, without the net loss of income and without an adverse effect on the poor. The rebated tax takes advantage of the efficiency of the market, but biases it in a desirable direction; and without necessitating a government bureaucracy that delves into people's lives; the tax could be collected from the producers and returned to consumers at income tax time.

A rebated tax on energy consumption would hit the affluent hardest. High-income groups could be hit hard by other changes, too, and this is especially true if we are not able to avoid falling into a deep recession. People who own stocks could see their value drop significantly (they already have seen their stocks devalued as the value of the dollar has fallen while the stock market has been unable to move steadily upward). If the value of real property falls, too, as during the Depression, renters would be the only ones to avoid financial losses. High-paid executives of large corporations could find themselves unemployed just as easily as wage earners, and they could find themselves totally inexperienced in other ways to earn a living. University professors are already being laid off as college enrollments sag and government budgets tighten.

However, on the basis of scarcity alone — as opposed to all the other factors that affect the economy — changes are apt to affect *industries* rather than *income classes.* Industries that are producing energy-expensive goods that are not essential (aluminum beverage containers for instance) will be adversely affected first, while those industries that produce energy, scarce raw materials, and essential goods should provide steady employment. As such, a drop in real income would affect people all across the class spectrum, not just working-class people and the poor.

There is very strong resistance to falling wages, an understandable reaction. This resistance takes many forms, but the most common one is the cost-of-living increase. It is almost assumed that take-home pay should be increased to cover increases in the cost of living. But to increase incomes to cover the rising costs of living denies the reality of scarcity since the higher income simply sustains existing consumption. It also discourages the process of substituting labor for materials. With cost-of-living increases, the labor cost to rehabilitate old buildings goes up with the cost of new construction; the cost of recycling scrap goes up with the value of the scrap; and the cost of labor goes up with the cost of equipment and energy, although perhaps not as fast. Unless we voluntarily reduce our consumption of energy — which we are not doing — some mechanism like higher prices or falling real incomes is the only way to force a drop in consumption.

The result of cost-of-living increases and higher incomes in a time of scarcity is "stagflation," the combination of unemployment and inflation. New jobs are discouraged by the high cost of labor, and inflation is caused by the continued heavy demand for scarce energy and raw materials that high incomes sustain. High incomes can be sustained for awhile, but not without creating imbalances that mean tougher times in the future. To overcome stagflation and reestablish balance in the economy requires a fall in income, a drop in consumption of raw materials, and a long, slow effort to establish viable new jobs which would have been established earlier if wages had been lower and raw materials more expensive.

This is the unpleasant point the environmental movement has reached. Gone are the heady enthusiasms of Earth Day, the hoped-for changes in politics, economics, and individual behavior. We did not restrain ourselves, so now it is a matter of letting scarcity do it by force through falling incomes and higher prices. The government, in essence, has no way to avoid the subsidence. This is the disagreeable business of environmental resistance making itself felt as the niche of industrial society begins to fill.

The Question of Employment

Falling incomes and higher prices are one thing, but unemployment is a much rougher business. It is possible to get by with less, but it is not possible to get by for long if one loses one's job altogether. If unemployment goes unchecked and there is increasing disparity in well-being between the employed and unemployed, it will pose a severe threat to political stability.

The traditional response to unemployment is to stimulate the economy by pumping in government cash to get consumers spending again in order to put workers back on the job. This approach was entirely appropriate in the past, and it was the great contribution of John Maynard Keynes in unravelling the riddle of the Great Depression — unemployed workers with abundant resources all around and idle factories. Cash had to be placed in workers' hands; then they had to be encouraged to spend it to get the factories going and the economy moving again. Federal deficits were the way to do this. But today, despite huge federal deficits, the rate of unemployment has remained high. Why is this the case?

The answer, if we accept the economic logic of scarcity, is the one that is familiar by now; with incomes at their present level and machines still profitable, new jobs are not opening up. Labor is not being substituted for energy and machines, as it should be. The jobs involved in developing new energy sources, for example, building solar devices, are not being created due to price controls on energy and high labor costs. Large, centralized manufacturers can still undersell small-scale producers because transportation remains cheap. Low prices for energy and machines continue to make it possible to process and transport agribusiness fruits and vegetables long distances so that small local truck farmers cannot make a living. Instead of permitting the economy to evolve in a more frugal direction and providing employment today, high wages and cheap energy have sustained affluence and exacerbated the problem of unemployment.

England provides the classic example of what happens when the government steps in and tries to maintain employment in declining industries. The profitable industries did not need help, and so the government bought only the declining ones as they started to go downhill. Once they were owned by the government, jobs were preserved and the losses mounted. To add to the imbalance, the wages of the unproductive jobs were pushed up, eventually causing a severe case of stagflation. As the value of the English pound fell, pressures were exerted by international monetary authorities to restrain the imbalance, but not before severe pressures were generated within English society, between classes, between regions, and even between different labor unions. It is a dangerous business, trying to deny an economic reality; it cannot be denied indefinitely without generating some pretty unpleasant social, political, and philosophical backlash.

The painful part is that the process of muddling toward frugality in America seems likely to entail increasing unemployment for some time to come. The precise level of unemployment will depend on a number of factors, but a major one is how rapidly energy becomes scarce. It takes time to shift jobs from declining sectors of the economy to those that are expanding. If plenty of time is available and the transition is smooth, unemployment may not increase. But the real consequences of the extravagant levels of consumption maintained in this country in the 1970s may well be a faster onset of scarcity, and with it higher unemployment. In any case, the level of unemployment will be one measure of how effectively we are adjusting to scarcity.

Let us look at one example. It is sometimes suggested that the best opportunity to reduce our use of imported oil would be to discourage unnecessary use of cars. Some estimates suggest that the use of cars could be cut by one-third by eliminating unnecessary trips, by carpooling, and by the greater use of public transportation. This sounds fine in the abstract, but were it to happen under today's economic conditions the effects would be very disruptive. Jobs would be lost in the auto industry as well as in the industries that supply its materials, such as steel, rubber, and glass. Jobs would also be lost in gasoline retailing and in all the service industries that are based on car travel, such as tourist facilities and the shopping centers reached by cars. As unemployed workers cut back on their expenditures, other workers would lose their jobs, in a "multiplier" effect. It is unlikely that the loss of so many jobs could be made up by new jobs in public transportation or by the opening of new shops that can be reached on foot or by bus. In short, the disruption caused by an abrupt cut in the gasoline consumed by cars is a good illustration of the undesirability of a "crash" program of this sort. It is far better to allow prices to rise slowly, permitting a steady adaptation to scarcity by everyone. To try to halt this steady rise in prices can lead to a series of much more severe problems, high unemployment being one of them. Once equilibrium in the economy is lost, it can be very hard to reestablish.

Even under the best of conditions, consider how awkward it will be to change to a more labor-intensive economy. As energy costs go up, labor will not immediately displace machines because of the capital already invested in the machines. When existing machines wear out, new ones may not be purchased, but until that occurs, the machines will still be used. There will be a delay in the creation of new jobs and that delay could push unemployment up significantly. At the same time, people in areas of declining employment will understandably be reluctant to leave their homes, families, and friends. People often prefer to remain in familiar surroundings even if it means greater economic distress to do so. In addition, workers with specialized skills for which the need is declining will be reluctant to start out again at an unskilled level. And everywhere, as reduced employment causes consumption to drop, the effect on other workers will multiply and could lead to a real depression if steps are not taken to head it off. At best it is a tricky business.

At the same time, it will be necessary to avoid the related pitfall of runaway inflation. There will be a general tendency for the government to favor inflation since it reduces the real burden of the national debt, which can then be serviced with deflated dollars. It is possible that federal deficits will grow larger because of inflation; but even so, a depression would be harder for government to deal with because it would reduce tax revenues and increase welfare expenditures so that servicing the national debt could become an insurmountable problem. Any tendency to favor jobs and inflation, however, will lead to increased stagflation and, if pushed too far, will ultimately result in a depression. A smooth transition to an economy based on frugality requires the avoidance of both depression and runaway inflation, thereby providing the stable economic environment that permits effective individual adaptation to increasing scarcity.

Even in the best of times, there are ups and downs in the economy. The period of resource scarcity we are entering will add new elements to further confuse economists trying to understand the economy and devise measures to maintain its stability. Because of scarcities, the upturns are likely to be more short-lived and the downturns longer and deeper than forecasts based on affluent years would suggest. When times are good, scarcity will be forgotten; but when the economy takes a downturn, people are likely to take a more pessimistic view of things than is necessary. Instability does not contribute to good forecasting and a smooth process of change.

One very desirable policy change could speed the transition to a more labor-intensive economy — the elimination of the current tax credit for investment and the expansion of the tax credit for the creation of jobs. The tax credit for investment was logical in the

past when there was much to gain by encouraging investment in labor-saving machinery. With an abundance of resources, the provision of labor-saving devices led to increased production and jobs. In times of
scarcity, however, the effect of the investment tax
credit is perverse in the extreme. It subsidizes the provision of machines that displace labor just when labor-
intensive work is needed, and it subsidizes resource-
consuming technology just when resources are getting
short. The tax credit for the creation of jobs, on the
other hand, subsidizes jobs at the expense of machines,
exactly the process needed both to help balance the expected job deficit and to discourage the consumption
of materials. Such a tax credit also encourages the development of the intermediate technology that E. F.
Schumacher calls for in *Small Is Beautiful,* technology
that is smaller in scale and accessible to the average
person.[8] Rarely are there policies available that have
such uniformly desirable effects as the job tax credit.
And on top of it all, there are excellent political prospects for expanding the tax credit and gaining wide acceptance. What politician would have the nerve to vote
against increased tax incentives for jobs and in favor of
maintaining incentives for big corporate investors?

Adam Smith or Thomas Jefferson?

The market system that Adam Smith described in
The Wealth of Nations was ideally suited to take advantage of the new opportunities created by the young

technology of the Industrial Revolution. The market offered powerful incentives to utilize the abundant resources that were available, to develop new products, to expand trade, and to establish markets worldwide. At the same time, the market system levied powerful penalties on traditional elements of society that simply wanted to preserve a way of life that was known and comfortable. More than any other social creation, the free market system can take credit for the dynamic character of the modern era.

But it is important that we challenge those who argue that the free enterprise system provides greater freedom than other ways of life. In actuality what it does is to substitute one set of constraints on the individual for another. In preindustrial society, the constraints were those of tradition, religion, and family; under the free enterprise system, the constraints are those established by the market. Thus, in our society an individual must obtain an education, must move to where work is available, and must compete vigorously to be successful, while in traditional society an individual had to fulfill traditional obligations to family and community in order to enjoy the respect of others. Whether one system offers more freedom than the other is a knotty question. Philosophers still argue about what freedom really is, but it seems entirely possible that the opportunity to be oneself within the constraints of an unchanging but supportive traditional culture may be a truer freedom than to live in the fluid and often threatening situations we find ourselves in today.

It is also important to bear in mind that the free market has forced us to act in some rather unpleasant ways. Hazel Henderson has remarked that at least four of the seven deadly sins of medieval Christianity are encouraged by the free market system — pride, envy, avarice, and gluttony; and the other three — anger, sloth, and lechery — may have some relation to the market economy as well. They are all unattractive qualities, and the sooner we can leave them behind us the better. That may not be for some time, unfortunately.

The operation of the market system, whatever its disadvantages, is still the only feasible mechanism to bring about the transition from an affluent society to a frugal one. The market will keep us honest, whether we like it or not, since it will be through the market that resource scarcity will make itself felt. The market will be the main force that keeps the consumer from squandering scarce resources, that forces producers to use labor rather than machines, and that keeps the government on the straight and narrow path between depression and runaway inflation. The market mechanism will weaken the bigness of American manufacturing and permit more individual- or family-sized enterprise. It will lead to the decentralization of the economy, to smaller scale technologies, to the repopulating of rural areas, and to reducing the overloading of our cities. The market will force us to do all the right things, even if for the wrong reasons. The government could help, but given the nature of American

democracy, government actions are more likely to op-
pose the subsidence rather than embrace it, since that
is what consumers and businesses both want. There
will be many efforts to deny the market, for reasons
that are both noble and selfish, but any effort that tries
to deny the reality of scarcity will eventually fail. The
society that grew and prospered under the market system now seems destined to subside under the same
system.

Until the inevitability of finite resources is accepted,
there is likely to be a great deal of political bitterness
and scapegoating. The peaking of affluence and the
initial decline will be the hardest time; we are probably
entering this period now. This is the time when the
market's role will be the most helpful, almost as a *deus
ex machina*. It will be easier and healthier to blame
impersonal market forces rather than any of the traditional scapegoats: capitalists, politicians, bureaucrats,
labor unions, blacks, Jews, welfare cheaters. And the
market will tell us how fast the subsidence must go, by
the rate at which raw material prices go up and work
opportunities change.

Later, when the reality of the new trends are understood and reluctantly accepted, people can be expected to start to reorganize their lives in some very
basic ways, to make life better and more secure, and to
move away from the vicissitudes of dependence on the
market. No one likes to have his job and the well-being of his family dependent on vast, impersonal
market forces over which he has no control. People

will begin to experiment with various forms of barter, cooperative arrangements among friends, and larger scale cooperative organizations — all designed to give people more control over their own lives. In the long run, as the momentum of modern economic society weakens, it can be expected that the market system will decline from the dominant position it has held since the eighteenth century and slowly be relegated to the subordinate place it has held in most societies — of facilitating the exchange of goods at the Saturday market, but not of ordering all of society.

Does this mean that Thomas Jefferson's pastoral ideal — of independent farmers, craftsmen, and merchants in self-governing communities — is to become a reality? In many ways it does; this is one of the most encouraging ways to envision the result of the subsidence. But since I have set myself the task of facing all the hard realities, it is important to mention that Thomas Jefferson's vision may not be complete. Jefferson, after all, was a part of the same philosophical movement as was Adam Smith, the movement known as the Enlightenment. It is more than mere coincidence that the Declaration of Independence was presented to the Continental Congress in the same year that *The Wealth of Nations* was published. Both men believed strongly in individual freedom; Jefferson in its political form, democracy; and Adam Smith in its economic form, the free market.

Yet, despite this congruence, Jefferson's vision of individual freedom was far from compatible with Adam

Smith's, or even with the way American democracy has
evolved. Jefferson's chief rival was Alexander Hamilton, a man who clearly reflected the ideas of Adam
Smith. It was Hamilton who shaped our country more
than any other single individual; he encouraged industrial development and also strong federal regulation.
Jefferson's pastoral ideal remained just that, an ideal
that did not have the power to resist the development
of industrial society in this virgin land. In his fine
book *The Machine in the Garden: The Pastoral Ideal
in America,* Leo Marx identifies Jefferson's crucial
weakness: his unwillingness to accept the necessity of a
structure in society strong enough to bring about the
good life he envisioned. Jefferson's understandable re-
vulsion with the corruption of eighteenth-century
Europe and the oppression of church and state led him
to reject these institutions; but Jefferson had also
traveled in England and rejected the "dark, satanic
mills" of the free enterprise system that he saw there.
His pastoral ideal was based, more than anything else,
on what remained of rural England — the age-old villages, fields, and woods — all the pleasant prospects
that attract tourists even today. In retrospect, Jefferson
must be charged with wishful thinking in proposing
that his "middle landscape," between the overripeness
of Europe and the primitiveness of the Indians, would
somehow evolve "naturally" in this country under a
mild form of government. The government was so
mild, in fact, that it was powerless to offer effective
resistance to industrialization.

What Jefferson saw in rural England was the remains of the medieval era; English society of that age
was a classic traditional society, with common operation of land under feudal ownership, strong religious
controls on individual appetites, and very limited mobility. Even though Jefferson liked what he saw in England, he was totally opposed to the way it was created.
He believed that the same final product could be obtained by the rational behavior of free individuals
acting in their own best interests, and without the unpleasant business of social constraints enforced by
some institution. It is this quality that still gives Jefferson his attractiveness today; we are still a frontier
people.

Yet, this very quality is bound up with the weakness
of Jefferson's vision. We seem to feel that we are somehow different from other people in other times, that we
do not need the ties that bound cultures together and
made them work. We feel we can have the best of both
worlds — a high degree of freedom and a rich community — without the mutual obligations and the limits
on individual behavior that gave other cultures their
distinctive character. The most recent effort to achieve
the Jeffersonian ideal was the commune movement of
the late 1960s and early 1970s, but the vast majority of
communes broke up quickly because of their inability
to provide the integration and commitment necessary
for any community to survive.

Perhaps, the very nature of the process of moving
toward frugality will work against the wish to return to

the freedom of the frontier. The frontier was, after all, the wide-open niche, the niche that is now filling up. Even in the past it was a pretty lonely place; individualism itself has recently been termed "the pursuit of loneliness."[9] Perhaps economic survival in the future will cause communities to pull together and to create common laws, "mutual coercion mutually agreed upon," in Garrett Hardin's phrase from "The Tragedy of the Commons."[10] Our passionately held individualism will have to give way to the practical realities of getting by without the surpluses that permitted us so much freedom in the past. After a while, we will cease to argue the pros and cons of the free market, of governmental regulation, of Adam Smith, or of Thomas Jefferson. It will have ceased to make any difference.

CHAPTER V

The Theory and Practice of Muddling

In 1959, Charles Lindbloom published a paper with the surprising title, "The Science of 'Muddling Through.'"[1] It dealt with the way administrators of large organizations actually make decisions, as opposed to the way textbooks and theorists say they should be made. There was quite a difference; the textbook approach is rational and comprehensive, while Lindbloom suggested that actual decisions are made by a simple coping behavior.

The textbook method of making decisions has all the qualities of an ideal approach. It starts with fundamentals — the tasks of establishing objectives and clarifying the values on which they are based. Once the objectives are clearly established, the various means to achieve them are identified and analyzed; all relevant factors are considered and the best theoretical knowledge applied. Finally, the policy that best achieves the desired objectives is selected. This approach to policy formulation was encouraged by the success of operations research and systems analysis in business and engineering, as well as in the methods of science. The student learning this approach was assured that he was learning how to make decisions with the greatest likelihood of success.

The only trouble is that this is rarely the way decisions are made, primarily because it is rarely possible. Once in a while a relatively simple issue can be handled with this degree of logic and straightforwardness, but usually the administrator finds that he rarely has the time, the information, the theoretical knowledge, or the intellectual capacity to make a rational, comprehensive decision. Worse yet, the administrator has to deal with conflicting objectives. For the business person, the engineer, or the scientist, a single objective can usually be established, but the public administrator confronts a whole range of mutually competitive public purposes. Even if the administrator starts with a single objective, this soon gives way to a number of competing objectives, and the final choice becomes more and more subjective. On top of that, numerous constraints are exerted on the administrator by elected officials, by client groups, and by the colleagues with whom the administrator works on a daily basis. The more deeply an issue is investigated, the more it becomes clouded with ambiguity. Pitfalls soon become apparent that could adversely affect the agency as well as the administrator's future. In all, the clear, open, rational, comprehensive method darkens into a quagmire of potential conflicts and hazards.

At this point, the administrator normally grasps desperately for something solid to hold onto, something he can base a decision on to protect himself and his agency. Invariably, he finds it in the results of past policy changes and in the advice of those most affected by the decision. Even with the best of intentions, the administrator ends up by taking only a modest step (well checked out with the powers that be), a step that at least makes a marginal contribution to the issue at hand. In the process of reaching a decision, the administrator becomes practical and political as well as rational. The result is muddling through.

Lindbloom went on to argue that the kind of real-life muddling through that characterizes administrative decision-making is the better way. These ideas subsequently converged with similar notions being explored in political science, and the result was the political theory of muddling through. It provides an excellent description of the political process as it actually works in this country. Even though it is far from ideal, it has many attractive qualities. At a time when politicians are widely condemned for problems that are more correctly understood as being rooted in the conflicts between increasing scarcity and our aspirations, the theory of muddling through is worth examining.

Muddling Toward the Public Interest

It is easy to see how Lindbloom's theory can be extended to the political process. Yet there is a great deal of resistance to accepting such a seemingly base view —

a view that is so cautious and full of compromise. Probably the most troubling criticism is that muddling along tends to preserve the status quo or, worse yet, the power elite, rather than identifying what is truly in the public interest and working toward it.

But what is the public interest? Walter Lippman once said that the public interest is "what men would choose if they saw clearly, thought rationally, and acted disinterestedly and benevolently."[2] That certainly sounds good, but as with the rational method of making decisions, it rarely can be carried out.

Let us look at each of Lippman's three criteria. The first, to see clearly the results of a political decision, is rarely possible. Who can really claim to know the effects of a guaranteed income, a mutual arms reduction pact, or a national health care program? Would a substantial tax on energy encourage a trouble-free reduction in the use of energy, or would it cause the economy to stumble into a depression? Certainly in the past, many consequences of public policy decisions were not clearly foreseen. Who could have known that aid to dependent children would force fathers from the house and increase illegitimacy; that urban renewal would turn out to be minority removal; that tax breaks for farmers would benefit corporate investors more than small farmers; or that the Viet Cong would be able to derail the American military machine? There is no question that politicians would certainly *like* to know the effects of proposed legislation; this is why they hold hearings and actually depend on lobbyists to tell them what special interest groups think the effects of a piece of legislation will be. But for every issue there will be many different opinions, and nothing can eliminate the potential hazard of being unable to see things correctly.

Lippman's second requirement, to think rationally, assumes that a clear goal exists and that data is available to evaluate alternative ways of reaching that goal. This is almost never the case. For the scientist, the goal is to increase knowledge, and data is obtained from highly controlled experiments, carefully designed to contribute to this goal. For the business person, the overriding goal is to make a profit, and a great deal of economic data is available that can contribute to this single objective. In the political process, by contrast, there are numerous conflicting goals — and little hard data. Equity, for example, is an important value, but it conflicts with the values of the free enterprise system, which requires inequality to motivate people; welfare is the classic case illustrating this conflict. Again, the preservation of the environment often conflicts with the preservation of jobs, as when the establishment of a national park puts miners or loggers out of business, or the closing of a polluting factory undermines the economic base of nearby towns. Politicians are rarely permitted the luxury of strongly held values because their constituency is rarely homogeneous enough to hold a single set of values. In the usual situation, the politician must try to support as many politically important, vote-getting issues as possible and to suggest that the conflicts that remain can be resolved through their own good political leadership. If a politician makes the mistake of taking firm stands on controversial issues, he will usually have his candor rewarded by not being reelected; the honest, straightforward politician alienates too many groups of voters. Some of the political values with the broadest voter support — full employment, higher incomes, lower prices, lower taxes, and less pollution — are in themselves contradictory. It is no wonder that a politician must try to be all things to all people and ends up appearing to have no values at all.

The third of Lippman's requirements, to act disinterestedly, is the most difficult and perhaps the least human. It suggests that we deny our upbringing, our experiences, our personality, and that we purge our minds and stop thinking. If each of us were elected representatives, it is certain that the way we would vote would be influenced by whether we were born in a big city, a small rural town, or suburbia; whether we were born wealthy or poor, white or black, were from a broken home or grew up in the extended family of an ethnic neighborhood; whether we lived through the Depression and World War II or have known only the postwar affluence. If a disinterested analysis were possible, would it be desirable? Perhaps, but such an approach also suggests a cold, mechanical sort of mind. Personally, I prefer real people with all their foibles and weaknesses -- as well as their talents, strengths, and unique imaginations.

Lippman's last requirement is that politicians act benevolently. But how is benevolence to be decided? If someone is judged as not acting benevolently, this usually means that the judge and the judged have different points of view. Is it more benevolent to help poor people by giving them welfare and perhaps making them dependent on such help, or not to provide help in the hope of forcing them to get back on their feet economically and in the end be better off for it? Who knows?

Lippman of course is not the only one to try to define the public interest. "The greatest good for the greatest number of people over the longest period of time" is another definition. Again it sounds fine, but in this case it is clearly impossible, especially as it applies to natural resources. If the greatest good is made of resources by the greatest number of people, the length of time that resources would be available must be reduced. The greatest good also may conflict with the greatest number of people, as when too many visitors to a national park diminishes the experience for all. Just as a family budget cannot at the same time maximize immediate expenditures for all members of the family and savings for the future, it is not theoretically possible for government to maximize the three variables of the greatest good for the greatest number of people over the longest time. One and often two must be sacrificed, and value judgments must be made. Making such judgments is what the political process does for us.

How does the theory of muddling through define the public interest? Muddling leads to the *due process* definition, which simply states that if a piece of legislation goes through the process established by the Constitution it is, therefore, in the public interest, *regardless of the nature of the legislation*. The due process definition is non-normative; its values are those of the process rather than any idea of right or wrong. The process is the key, and it is a tortuous one: legislation must be introduced in both houses of Congress, go through the appropriate committees, be passed by both houses (the difference resolved in a conference committee), be signed by the president or vetoed (the veto to be overridden by a two-thirds vote of both houses), and, finally, the law must not be successfully challenged in the courts as a violation of the Constitution. The process provides ample opportunities for opponents or supporters to make themselves heard; it does not give excessive power to the executive, legislative, or judiciary branch of government; it protects individual rights. If a piece of legislation makes its way through this cumbersome process without being scuttled by opponents, it is then — from the perspective of muddling through — considered to be in the public interest, regardless of what any particular individual or group may feel about it.

In actual practice, any measure that is highly controversial rarely gets through. If it is anything, the process of muddling through is cautious; it is one long series of compromises that rarely satisfies any one group. The "perfect" compromise is the one that all interest groups are equally dissatisfied with. But with muddling, we at least avoid the big mistakes of stronger forms of government — such as China's Great Leap Forward that floundered, the forced sterilization that contributed to Indira Gandhi's downfall in India, or Russia's virgin lands program. We may not have many smashing achievements that thrill the whole country, but we do not have the huge failures either.

So far nothing has been said about the role of the individual in all this, except as a voter. The role of the voter is, of course, a key role and is the prod that keeps the politician on the track. But beyond that the individual's role in the muddling process of government is minimal. Muddling through is preeminently a *group process*. In a practical sense, with over two hundred million people in this country, an individual cannot carry much weight, nor can a politician respond to bits and pieces of information from many individuals. Only by pooling one's influence in a politically active group can the individual hope to have some impact.

When the representative of an interest group appears before a congressional hearing, the political process is receiving organized inputs that can be responded to and evaluated. When a spokesman for General Motors testifies before a committee, he is listened to, not because he speaks for the power elite but because he represents a corporation that has some half million employees and 1.4 million stockholders. That is a lot of voters, and the members of Congress

want to know how General Motors feels about a measure that affects so many people. Conservation groups
are no different. They publish their membership figures regularly, and when appearing before congressional committees their representatives make it clear
whom they represent. No congressman wants to get on
the wrong side of the conservationists. Each election
year conservation groups pool their resources and iden-
tify the "dirty dozen," twelve congressmen who have
the worst voting record on conservation issues, and
each time a number of those congressmen do not get
reelected. The point is this: so-called special interests
must exist to make sure that politicians are aware of all
the multitudinous demands of the population they are
serving. If special interests do benefit excessively from
the political process, it is usually because opposing
forces are weak or not present at all. Maritime ship-
ping interests, for example, receive large subsidies primarily because no one is harmed by them — only the
Treasury suffers.

In most cases, however, the job of being a politician
and responding to a constituency is exceedingly tough.
Most major issues have at least two sides and often
there are more, and no matter which way the politician votes, he is likely to offend some influential
groups. A politician would prefer to sit securely on the
fence between two sides, delay the day of judgment,
and pray that someone will come up with a compromise that may make no one happy yet offends no one.
Sometimes this happens; sometimes the problem dis-

appears; sometimes events move ahead and make the decision clear. But just as often a vote is taken that causes one side of an issue to announce that politicians are corrupt, despicable characters who have sold out to "special interests."

Those more experienced in the political process realize that this is not the case. "Special interests" are in fact legitimate interests of different groups involved with a given issue. Most elected representatives have very little flexibility in coping with the multiple forces that determine who stays in office. Caution comes first — to hold onto one's elected seat — and it is rare that a politician is secure enough and powerful enough to go much beyond that. Democracy, after all, is a representative form of government; politicians are elected to do what their *constituencies* want them to do, more than what they themselves would do if they had the freedom to do it.

The elected officials of conservation groups face some of the same constraints as elected governmental officials. Conservation groups would like to be able to speak for several million members rather than several hundred thousand, and so they often get pulled into the same game as the politicians — the game of trying to be all things to all potential members and avoiding controversial positions that may alienate people. For example, conservation groups rarely call for programs that would restrain mobility, since their members are highly mobile, enjoying outings all around the United States and even the world. Conservation organizations

seem hesitant to endorse higher prices for energy as a
conservation measure since higher prices are not popular. It is safer to show photographs of forests devastated
by loggers or telephoto shots of polluted cities, and to
call for abstractions such as strong regulations, force-
ful planning, and changes in values rather than for
specific policies that reduce consumption, restrict mobility, or raise taxes or prices.

Politicians must weigh all the information they receive from interest groups; they cannot just count
heads on both sides of an issue. In retrospect, the modest size of the Redwood National Park was not surprising, once the major arguments were heard. The conservation organizations could muster a nationwide
constituency for the park, and everyone had seen the
before and after photographs of majestic redwood forests turned into a stubble field of blackened stumps by
logging companies. But the local people in the several
counties in Northern California where redwoods are
logged, whose numbers were a fraction of the park
supporters nationwide, still could say, rightly or
wrongly, "Here are these environmentalists, affluent
city people compared to ourselves, who have everything and now propose to come up here and put us out
of work to preserve their summer playground; sustained yield is not possible if logged or unlogged land is
taken out of production." In effect, one lost job is
weighed considerably heavier than one disappointed
conservationist. In this case a unique compromise was
reached, the kind of compromise that politicians like.

When $359 million was approved for the expansion of the park, $40 million was also provided for income maintenance of workers displaced from the lumber industry. Again, only the Treasury suffers.

The Benefits of Muddling

If there are conflicts in the political system, they are between the legitimate differences of the various groups concerned with specific issues. To the spokesmen for specific industries, regions, labor unions, conservation groups, minorities, and radicals of all colors, the issues are clear. But to the politician surveying the scene, it is not clear at all. The genius of our political system is that it provides an arena for the controlled conflict of competing values and ideas. It permits the resolution of conflicts without civil war. Only on the issue of slavery was the process not up to the test; but the United States has a good record for two centuries, better than the record of almost all other countries. France now has its fifth republic, and the directness of the English parliamentary system has allowed policy to take wider swings left and right as Labor and Conservatives exchange power. Elsewhere in the world, there is a tendency for "strongmen" to take over governments, and one of their justifications for this is the squabbling of political parties and the inefficiencies of open political processes. Yet, without the stabilizing inefficiences of conflicting special interests and compromise, autocratic governments inevitably stray too far left or right and generate the inevitable counter-coup, necessitating a police state to maintain the government by force — all of which, mercifully, we are spared. Such are the advantages of inefficiency.

Whenever there is an attempt to set up an ideal government agency, one that is designed to transcend the presumed baseness of "politics as usual," the result is often a failure. City planning provides a good example. City planning has traditionally been set up as a professional staff function and isolated from "political interference." The idea is that planners are trained for their jobs and know what they are doing, while politicians do not; the planners will do what is right rather than what is politically expedient. But there is general agreement that the results of city planning efforts have been largely unsuccessful. First, to try to isolate planners from the political process is impossible, since politicians must put into effect the plans that planners come up with. Politicians will not do this if the political sense that keeps them in office tells them that the public does not like the plan (if it is too expensive, threatens jobs, is too radical a change, etc.). Second, planners, like their close kin, architects, often seem more interested in creating impressive monuments that will get them awards in professional journals than in listening to the everyday concerns of people living in cities. Much of New York's financial trouble today stems from the grand schemes of planner par excellence Robert Moses, while Chicago, with its machine politics and ward captains, is in better shape. Isolating planners from the political process (like isolating any government activity) does not work, primarily because it is undemocratic.

In sum then, the process of muddling through is a gutsy, down-to-earth process full of inefficiencies and inconsistencies. It takes an inordinate amount of time to take modest incremental steps forward, and significant bold steps are clearly not in the cards. The process can be a lot of fun for those who enjoy it and do not take themselves too seriously — the politician who loves to talk to people, the lobbyist who thrives on finding ways to gain access to the influential, or the activist who enjoys organizing people. It keeps this country pretty close to the middle of the road, while still permitting slow, faltering adjustments to change. All the jibes about our political process seem pretty appropriate. Ralph Waldo Emerson said democracy was "a raft which would never sink, but then your feet are always in the water." E. B. White defined it as "the recurrent suspicion that more than half the people are right more than half the time." I rather like Plato's definition of democracy as "a charming form of government, full of variety and disorder, and dispensing a sort of equality to equals and unequals alike." Democracy may not be an inspired form of government, but no one has found anything better; and even those most dissatisfied with it would never agree on an alternative.

CHAPTER VI

The Hazards of Muddling
Toward Frugality

At this point, the reader may want to say, "Okay, muddling may be all right when times are good and there is not much hanging in the balance — the times when people seem to get by well no matter what the government does. But what if things got tough, and we really needed a strong, effective government? Wouldn't a muddling sort of government just make things worse?" And things may very well get tough, as Robert Heilbroner has pointed out so well in *An Inquiry into the Human Prospect*.[1] If government is incapable of providing effective leadership, doesn't this suggest that the future will be much tougher than it would otherwise have to be?

There is no question that there are real dangers in muddling toward a way of life based on renewable resources. Any change of such a magnitude is bound to strain the bonds that hold a society together, even if plenty of time is available in which to make the change. But I find it hard to imagine that the real hazards are those most frequently mentioned or that

the political process is not up to the task or that the
absence of effective federal leadership is an ominous
failing Let us consider this last point of view before
looking at what are probably the real hazards.

The Imagined Hazards of Muddling Through

Detractors of our political process say it has survived
because it enjoyed the luxury of two centuries of growing abundance; the job of dividing up a pie that is
growing larger is a pleasant job, since everyone gains at
least something. There is undoubtedly some truth in
this, but there have been hard times as well; change is
never easy, even when it involves growth. It has not
been the age of peace and plenty that might have been
expected to accompany such rapid material progress.
The Depression was a severe jolt, and it was especially
unsettling since it was so hard to comprehend. There
was a growth of radicalism, but most people accepted
the hard times with fortitude, even if they were
dispirited. The direct, clear challenge of World War II
was almost a relief compared to the perplexities and
inaction of the Depression years. And even the long
period of prosperity that followed the war had its share
of disturbances, both national and international. The
most difficult of these was the Vietnam War, which
caused deep divisions in our society.

The Vietnam War is a painful example of what can
happen when the president can bypass the political
process and act directly as commander-in-chief of the

armed forces. President Eisenhower made the first fatal step into the quagmire of Vietnam, and subsequent presidents dutifully followed, always relying on misplaced patriotism to maintain the momentum behind the war. But after great loss of life and much frustrated opposition, the majority of the American people finally said, "No more." The political process was able to bring the country to the agonizing decision to pull out, even though it took a long time to reach the decision; by the time it was made there was no question that it was the right one. By the time we left Vietnam, the writing was so clearly on the wall that all but a few were able to read it. If the decision had been made earlier, there might have remained the disturbing thought that had we pushed on, the war could have turned out all right. As it was, we learned our lesson well; we will be very careful not to follow the same pattern. There are indications that, as we move toward the last part of this century, we are beginning to learn some important lessons in the same painful way: Affluence cannot increase indefinitely; technology does not have an answer for all shortages; the march of progress may be taking us in the wrong direction. *The big advantage of the resource issues we are facing is that they are less ambiguous than those of the Depression or the Vietnam War.* Shortages are real, in hard, physical terms. And even though skeptics will try to deny them by suggesting that they are contrived by big corporations, and even though some of the technological questions are still not answered, the writing on the wall is steadily becoming clearer. Wishful thinking will always remain, and the media will continue to report a geologist's musings as the equivalent of a new oil field and the inventor's dream as all but reality. But such efforts at escapism will increasingly be overwhelmed by the reality of scarcity. As the public accepts these realities, so will their elected representatives.

But what about the matter of national planning? To my mind, the call for national planning more and more sounds like the echo at the bottom of the barrel. Otherwise, those making the call would, instead, be calling for specific measures; this is the way we have always responded in the past. But, when there are no measures that are clearly desirable, an abstraction — planning — is called for to magically get us back on the path (even though this country has long been hostile to planning compared to European and Third World countries). The painful, unrewarding business of dealing with specific problems can be swept under the rug of planning; the government will presumably go after scarcity as it went after the moon landing, hiring a lot of engineers and putting plenty of people to work on it, but letting the rest of the country get on about its business with only superficial adjustments. The political recognition that anything more may be involved is so painful to politicians, consumers, and industries alike that it may be some time before it is fully accepted. No politician wants to acknowledge the inevitability of higher prices or falling real incomes or, worse yet, to admit there is little he can do to stop it.

In order to be effective, planning would have to accept the reality of this oncoming scarcity. It is hard to say how long it will be before this happens, how long before the wishful thinking about resources begins to lead us into greater problems. The analogy with Vietnam is a very good one here. While the war was going on, there was a great deal of planning effort and discussion of strategies. But once the decision to withdraw was made, the issue was immediately simplified — how to get out with the least amount of additional loss. Similarly, once we give up the effort to keep the economy growing, the policy questions will immediately become much simpler. No longer will we be asking planners to provide us with a miracle, to sustain economic growth as resources become scarcer.

And as with Vietnam, the final acceptance of frugality will not be as difficult as we expect, especially as the effort to prop up a declining affluence causes more and more economic and political backlash. Once the decision is made, our economic problems will be greatly simplified. The main task will be to dismantle the governmental paraphernalia built up over the years to encourage growth and the use of resources. That should be fairly easy. They could be replaced with a handful of policies to encourage labor-intensive work and discourage resource consumption. But even these will not be essential as long as the market is allowed to provide the signals for individual adaptation. New policies can be introduced at a leisurely pace, as the spirit moves us. Most important, initially, is the elimination of the pro-growth programs which are distorting the market mechanism.

In these days when we still have hopes of winning the war against scarcity, I suppose there is no harm in hiring a small army of planners to work on energy, economics, and so on. Assuming that planners will be as ineffective as they usually are — especially since they will be working on an impossible task — it should not cause too much harm. Since they will have to offer a fancy product in order to sell it to Congress, they may succeed in creating a degree of complacency for a while, and that would be unfortunate. Then again, the absence of miraculous results would help to dispel the last of any wishful thinking about the ability of government to find an easy solution to this difficult problem. One possible danger connected with the planning effort is the situation in which a very aggressive planning effort would somehow lock us into plans that prevent the kind of individual adaptation to scarcity that is already beginning. But this is highly unlikely; it would be uncharacteristic of Congress to go along with a strong planning operation since Congress would have to give too much power to the planners. Congress likes to be able to make decisions itself as the political winds change.

The Real Hazards of Muddling Through

While some hazards seem to me to be insubstantial, there are some real hazards in muddling toward frugality. They come not from the political process as a whole, but from the efforts of individuals and groups to maintain their advantages at the expense of others. The political process will be the main avenue for the exercise of group self-interest.

As the economic pie grows smaller, the natural tendency will be for everyone to try to maintain the size of his own piece. Obviously, everyone cannot do this, and to the degree that some are successful, antagonisms and hostilities would be generated. Worst of all, if some coalition of powerful interests were able to take us too far from a reasonable path in which we all shared the burdens of change fairly, it could generate a violent attempt to redress the balance. A situation of this sort would be ripe for the demagogue or the fanatic to capitalize on, and if such an imbalance were created and hardened into permanence, it could divide the country bitterly. What is needed, of course, is not a rigid defense of self-interest, but free-flowing adaptation.

Large industries are always assumed to be the ones to gain special advantages because of their wealth and power. At present, they certainly seem to be able to do this with fair success, largely because there are jobs — and votes — at stake. But if the large, centralized manufacturing operations weaken in the future, so will their political clout. Many industries that are considered essential now, even, for example, the automobile industry, could decline significantly as the cost of cars and gasoline climbs steeply and incomes stagnate.

Moreover, cooperation within an industry to maintain
prices is not likely at a time when demand is weakening
since high prices would further depress sales. Even an
out-and-out monopolist, who can set prices at will,
does not necessarily make a profit; control of the alu-
minum-can market in the future would not be worth
very much — about as much as control of the buggy
whip industry would be worth today.

Those industries dealing with essentials such as food,
energy, and raw materials will be much stronger. But
the tendency so far has been for the political process to
control those industries tightly. Since necessities are
likely to use up a larger part of household expenditures,
there is certain to be persistent and widespread political pressure to resist any unfair price increases. If recent experience is any indication, in fact, the tendency
may be to overcontrol prices to the point of sustaining
excessive consumption.

Certainly, large corporations will not be as secure
from the perils of competition as they are today. As
costs for transportation increase, the small, decentralized producers will start to enjoy improvements in their
relative competitive position. The large firms that are
tied into the heavy use of transportation, energy, and
machinery (the inputs that will be increasingly expensive) will see their power erode. Even those industries
that produce necessities will have to deal with the competition from small, flexible, labor-intensive local
producers. The best thing about small-scale solar or
wind power, firewood, methane digesters, bicycles,

and farm horses is that they all will help break the power of the big energy corporations. Any contrived advantage the big corporations may gain will soon turn counterproductive, for such gains will simply encourage the use of renewable resources.

There will, of course, be many attempts by government to help industries, not so much to maintain corporate profits as to preserve jobs. Depression will be pictured as the alternative. And whereas direct subsidies will be unlikely, all sorts of indirect assistance will be sought — through taxes, regulations, or loan guarantees. There will be a lot of high-powered thought put into these matters, as there has always been, and many ingenious devices will be invented. Some of the first industrial casualties are likely to receive assistance of one sort or another. But this assistance is not apt to be extended very widely since the cost to the government or the consumer could rapidly get out of control. Sooner or later, such industries will be on their own.

Some labor groups will have a stronger hand to play, though not the industrial unions; they will face the same obstacles as their corporate employers, and an increase in wages will only increase the price of the product, reduce sales, and eliminate jobs. But many municipal unions have a stranglehold on the functioning of cities, and they are in a much stronger position to strike for higher wages. Yet, if they were to press their advantage too far against the already strong political opposition, it could provoke a taxpayers' revolt. Or alternatively, high taxes and poor services would only serve to accelerate the flight from the cities that is already occurring. As is the case so frequently, pushing an immediate advantage reduces long-term advantage.

Everywhere we look, there are real constraints on the efforts of groups to obtain something at the expense of others. But it is a messy process, and it is hazardous.

Government employees, being somewhat removed from the market, may be able to go against the trend a little longer. Still, there is a limiting factor here too — the decline in tax revenue that will follow the decline in corporate and personal incomes. The ability of local governments to borrow is already restricted in some states and cities that are heavily in debt, and the same constraint is likely to affect the federal government, too, sooner or later. So far, cities with financial problems, such as New York, have responded by laying off workers rather than trimming salaries. This reduces the level of service and transfers a good part of the financial burden to state and federal unemployment and welfare programs.

I often wonder how the employees of a government agency would respond to a proposal that, in the face of impending layoffs, stated that all employees should take a cut in pay (and hours of work, to soften the blow), in lieu of laying off the employees with least seniority. Acceptance of such a proposal would signify the acceptance of frugality, less income, less consumption, and the need to spread available work more widely. The proposal would probably generate antagonism be-

tween junior and senior employees. The younger people, who ordinarily are the first to go, are the ones who
are finding it so hard to get a job in the first place, and
even if they do find a job, couples cannot afford to buy
a house or to start a family with only one salary. The
senior people, on the other hand, have much more job
security, as well as higher incomes and homes purchased
at a fraction of current prices, and their families are
well on their way. But with their greater security, they
are not likely to go along with a work reduction in lieu
of a layoff. Even when the writing is clearly on the
wall, it says different things to different people. The
substantial economic differences between well-established senior employees and younger workers could be
one of those imbalances that cause widespread dissatisfactions in the future.

Government, business, and labor do not operate independently of each other, and their goals are not
necessarily antagonistic. A strong industry means that
its labor is happy, as are its executives and financial
backers. A government bureau will be stronger if it is
involved with a strong industry rather than a declining
one. This symbiotic relationship between business, labor, and government is often noticed in agriculture,
aviation, and the military. If it is effectively exercised
by one industry, such mutual aid could give that industry a significant advantage over other industries, providing a substantially larger share of a declining
economic pie. But as long as such an arrangement occurred in just one industry, that industry would not be

able to resist the political antagonism that would inevitably develop; and the correction of the inequality, when it occurred, would probably be applied with a vengeance. In any case, it is very hard to imagine a single segment of the economy that could hold the rest of the country at ransom.

Could a broader alliance be formed that not only could gain an excessive share of the national wealth but sustain itself politically? Such an alliance was what the labor movement in England felt it had, after its election victories of 1964 and 1974. Out of its centuries-old antagonism to the upper classes, labor tried to push its wages up faster than did other groups in England. Any group that is strong enough to maintain political support for a strategy like this is also too large to benefit from it; it is not possible for a large piece of the pie to grow when the pie itself is shrinking. The result in England was severe inflation and unemployment. Only a minority could benefit economically from such a trick, but the political process is effective in restraining a group of this size. Between the workings of the market and the political process, we should be safe. In the end, the number of attempts made by groups, large or small, to gain advantage will determine how "rough" politics will be and, ultimately, how dangerous.

Some inequalities are bound to arise, and, to a degree, they are desirable. Workers must be encouraged to leave declining industries; this is brought about by declining wages as well as a declining number

of jobs. Similarly, relatively high wages may be necessary to attract workers to some less attractive industries
and work sites. For example, a good part of our coal
resources are in the northern Great Plains, not exactly
the bright lights capital of the country or the region
with the most comfortable winter weather. In 1976,
the states with the lowest unemployment rates were
Nebraska, Kansas, South Dakota, Iowa, and Wyoming,
in that order — all states with agriculture, coal, or
both. Their unemployment rates were all less than half
of most industrial states.

In all periods, some industries gain and others lose.
In the past, manufacturing, retail trade, and services
gained while agriculture and raw materials declined;
in the future, it looks as if it will be the other way
around. The amount of inequity in wages will be a
good indication of the rate of change required. Let us
hope the inequities are not so great that destructive
forces are generated; rapid change is a dangerous
thing.

Like industries, governments wax and wane. The
last century has seen the federal government grow
steadily until now it leaves to state and local governments only the details of carrying out federal policies.
Washington has taken on all the important economic
questions and regulates most phases of life in this country. The key that gave so much power to the federal
government was the constitutional authority to regulate interstate commerce. Since virtually all goods now
cross state lines in our highly integrated economy, the

federal government can regulate everything pertaining to manufacture, sale, and consumption. The federal graduated income tax with its built-in escalator clause provided continually increasing revenues to fund an activist, federal government, while the state and local governments were left to struggle with lagging revenues from property and sales taxes. But as incomes fall and the economy decentralizes, federal dominance will weaken. More significantly, if economic stagnation occurs, federal revenues will fall faster than state and local revenues.

The federal government will certainly be important for as long as it is reasonable to look ahead in the process of muddling toward frugality. Still, its period of expansion may be approaching its zenith. The type of economy we are heading for will involve a much more intricate adaptation to local environments, and regulation will necessarily be more of a job for state and local governments. Federal policies applied across the board nationwide will soon become much too crude and heavyhanded, and the logic for decentralization of governmental authority will gain favor. Only if a highly centralized source of energy, such as breeders or fusion, were successful (an increasingly unlikely prospect) would economic decentralization fail to occur. Then we would be forced to continue playing the political game on the vast scale and with the high stakes that exist today.

In short, there are political hazards in making the transition to a simpler, more sustainable way of life;

that much can surely be agreed upon. But the question remains: How serious are they? Many people assume that if we started to run out of resources the political consequences would be violent. Will we or our children have to go through a conflagration of some kind, with a harsh, emotionally devastated existence rising out of the ashes? What are the possibilities that the transition will be abrupt rather than smooth?

It is, of course, impossible to say. But to my way of thinking, it appears that we have reasons to be optimistic. We have a constitutional system which, because of its unique characteristics, has a long history of successfully resolving conflicts and de-fusing issues that have led to violence in other countries. Perhaps "resolving" conflicts is not the correct word; perhaps it is more correct to say that our political process deals with them so cautiously and inefficiently, and is so prone to compromise, that it simply discourages revolutionary movements. Rather than leading, the government is more correctly described as following — legitimizing changes once they have become acceptable to the public. As long as the political process can continue to dispense its rough sort of justice and stay pretty close to the safest possible place — squarely in the middle of the road — it should be able to do the job that is needed. It by no means assures us of a smooth transition, but there is certainly no reason to assume that people will immediately turn to violence if things get tough.

Rather than try to bring about fundamental changes in our political system (changes that never get far anyway), the trick will be to maintain the proven resilience of the system we have. How can this be done? I would refer back to the difference between the comic and the tragic perspective described in Chapter I.

If we maintain our sense of humor, and accept the world as it is and endeavor to make the most of it, then I would say that we should have no fears about the future. What governments do, after all, depends more than anything else on the pressures put on elected officials by voters and special interest groups. The political process will be a good indicator of how sensible we are and what kind of public temperament we create. There will inevitably be intemperate language, and self-righteous demands hurled in all directions. If we shrug them off and go about our lives, our elected representatives will do the same. There is no single group powerful enough to bend the country to its evil will, no single leader strong enough to lead millions of people somewhere they do not want to go, and no way to blame politicians for the ills of the country. As has always been true, we will get the kind of government we deserve.

Ultimately, the issue comes down to a matter of individual responsibility. If we accept that our well-being depends on what we ourselves do — how well we cope with the changes that are occurring around us — rather than on what someone in government is presumably doing for us, things will go better. The people who go about the task of doing what they can to secure a safe, comfortable — if frugal — niche and who develop stable ties with family, friends, and community will be doing the right thing. In that way, politics will tend to become the small-scale, face-to-face process that Jefferson idealized.

CHAPTER VII

The Pace of Change

A decentralized way of life based on the careful use of renewable resources is certainly feasible in the United States, there is no question of that. The ratio of population to land and resources is far better here than in most other countries in the world, and we have advanced technology, good communications, and high levels of education. Despite all our advantages, however, there is one thing that could derail the process of moving toward frugality — and that is having to do it too quickly. The transition is not just a matter of values and attitudes. There is a great deal of rebuilding to do; we have to beat our industrial complexes into plowshares, into different tools appropriate for a different kind of economy. And for this we need time.

Under any circumstances, the changes involved will not be easy. But if they must occur rapidly as well, an impossible situation could result. What could force such an abrupt change? — the rapid depletion of a key resource, a cutoff of imported oil, a major depression, a breakdown in the international monetary system, or

some form of international conflict that interrupts
trade. Any of these could accelerate the subsidence
mercilessly, even destructively, and the result would reflect the process by which it was reached — a major
discontinuity rather than a smooth evolutionary process. There would be bitterness and hostility inherent
in such harsh circumstances. The change would not be
something that people created by their own decisions
in response to changing conditions and in the context
of evolving cultural alternatives. Even the people who
are voluntarily opting for a simpler way of life would
not feel the same about it if they were forced to accept
it immediately, without time to plan and prepare.

The Social Costs of Rapid Change

When President Ford was in office his energy pro-
posals were quite similar to President Carter's later on,
except for one basic difference. Ford emphasized energy *development* as well as conservation, while Carter
emphasized *conservation* primarily. Ford proposed
that oil and gas prices be decontrolled, to let higher
prices discourage consumption and encourage production. Carter, on the other hand, proposed that taxes be
used to bring up energy prices, which would discourage consumption but not provide incentives to energy
producers, since the extra revenue would go to the government instead of to industry.

The difference did not seem especially significant at
the time, and Congress had its own ideas in any case,

but the difference in the two approaches, if carried out, would have played a significant role in determining the pace of change. The consequences of two hypothetical policies, development and conservation, are shown in Figure 2. Developing energy resources now would minimize change in the immediate future by bringing more oil and gas into the market. but would require a more abrupt and dangerous rate of change later on when these premium fuels were depleted. The assumption behind the development policy, of course, is that technological breakthroughs would take over as oil and gas supplies gave out, but this is a risky assumption. There is no assurance that it is correct. The policy of conservation, on the other hand, assumes that alternatives to oil and gas will be inferior in terms of price and quantity available, and that more effort to reduce consumption is needed now to reduce the potential of a severe hazard later. It is the more conservative policy, and if it is wrong, no great harm will result.

The first part of Figure 2, from 1950 to 1975, shows actual energy consumption for those years. The portion supplied by domestic oil and gas is the shaded portion, and it is continued into the future by using M. K. Hubbert's projection of remaining oil and gas (previously referred to on page 80) to indicate the rapidly declining role that domestic oil and gas is likely to play. Even with maximum conservation, the amount of energy that will have to be made up by imported oil, coal, and other domestic sources is intimidating. The

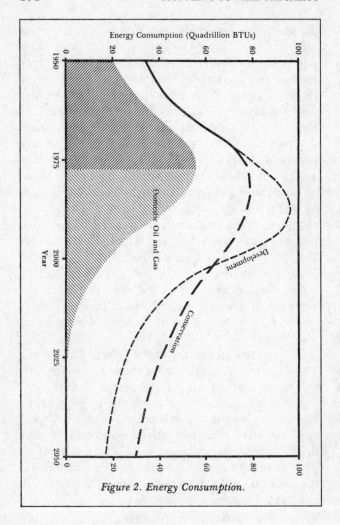

Figure 2. Energy Consumption.

THE PACE OF CHANGE

rapid increase in the use of energy between 1950 and 1975 and the scale of our present use, compared to oil and gas resources, are both apparent. To pull out all the stops now in a push for more energy supplies could be disastrous later on. To the degree that energy supplies were greatly expanded, the likelihood of the rapid decline of energy available later would be dramatically increased. As a result of trying to maintain business-as-usual, far greater disruption would be caused.

The two projections shown, for development and conservation, are purely hypothetical. There are too many unknowns to be more precise. The performance of the economy, the rate of development of coal, and the decisions made by oil exporting countries would all have an effect. Given what we do know, however, the conservation projection would seem to be manageable and could provide a smooth transition to frugality. The rate of decline would be half as fast as the growth of the last twenty-five years. It would then stabilize somewhat during the next coal era. Is it too optimistic or too pessimistic to suggest that in 2050 energy consumption will be roughly the same as in 1950? But this is the pace of change that would not put intolerable burdens on society, that would allow time to experiment and to build, and that would enable those who are reluctant to change to stay where they are even if their level of affluence were to decline.

If it were possible to maintain historic growth rates for a decade or two, based on an aggressive effort to develop all sources of readily available energy, a pre-

cipitous drop would be much more likely to occur later
in this century and early in the next. Impossible demands would be made on the economy, the political
system, and, indeed, on our entire social fabric. To
discourage such thinking, it is instructive to consider
what it might be like to go through such an "overshoot-
collapse" experience.

Frugality with a Vengeance

It takes time to replace machines and energy with labor, to decentralize economic activity, and to replace
dying industries with new ones. It takes time that
would not be available if energy supplies dropped
abruptly. On a theoretical basis, the loss of jobs caused
by energy scarcity would be balanced by new jobs in
labor-intensive, decentralized work. But on a realistic
basis, it is very hard to imagine this changeover happening so neatly; there would almost certainly be a lag
in the creation of new jobs. Firms would be more apt to
just lay off employees, especially in the face of all the
uncertainties inherent in such a fluid situation.

It would also take time for individuals to go into
some form of independent economic activity, to develop skills, to obtain tools, and to find a market. During
the Depression, men sold apples on street corners because nothing else was feasible. Circumstances had become a trap. This could occur again if an economic re-
versal were to hit a city or a region especially hard. It
would trap the people where they are.

One prominent example could be the automobile industry around Detroit, with all its suppliers and the retail trade that depends on paychecks from the auto industry. If the demand for cars were to slump, the money flowing into this region would diminish tremendously. Many of the people who lost their jobs would try to sell their homes in order to move elsewhere, but there would be few buyers; it would be necessary to sell a house for a low price in order to sell it at all, and the housing market could fall heavily. The modest amounts of money available from unemployment or welfare would not be adequate for breadwinners to leave their families with enough money to live on while they searched for jobs elsewhere in the country. Offering to work for lower wages would help a bit, but not much, since it would be the shortage of energy that would primarily be depressing the demand for cars, rather than labor costs. If other work were found, it would likely be intermittent or menial labor. Rural areas might offer some opportunities, but housing would be scarce, especially for a family. Caught in such a situation, a family would be more apt to try to sit it out, to sell what they could, to have anyone in the family get whatever work he could, and to hope the economic situation would pick up. But if energy continued to get scarcer, the energy-intensive industries never would pick up, and the stage would be set for a permanent class of unemployed, trapped individuals.

Unemployment on a large scale would almost surely overload welfare systems and would bankrupt state unemployment funds, some of which are already in the red. The fall in economic activity would cause tax revenues to fall and claims for compensation to increase. If unemployment ever reached the levels of the Depression, with some one-fourth of the work force without jobs, federal benefits would have to fall if the government were to remain solvent.

Instability would be a pervasive consequence of rapidly declining energy supplies. Uncertainties and disruptions would almost certainly cause prices to fluctuate, perhaps wildly. Scarcity might initially push prices up, but if unemployment caused consumption to fall off significantly, prices could come tumbling back down. In such a situation, the job of planning by business people would become more one of gambling than anything else. Their profit or loss would be determined more by the prices of what they bought and sold than by whether they were producing efficiently or increasing their use of labor instead of machines and energy. Some business people would be lucky and make a huge profit, while others would hit it wrong and go bankrupt, contributing unnecessarily to unemployment. Similarly, sudden high prices for a particular material might generate investments to produce it, only to have prices fall again a short time later, closing the new plant and wasting the scarce capital that went into it. Spectacular fluctuations in prices also attract speculators who, if they purchase materials in short supply, cause prices to rise further and further increase scarcity. But for most business activities, fluctuating prices are a measure of uncertainty, and the usual response of the business person is the same as the unemployed worker — to sit tight until the economic situation stabilizes and to wait until it becomes easier to see where things are going.

The worst thing about such fluctuations is that, once started, they tend to continue, shifting irregularly from one extreme to the other. The tools available to the government to dampen them are crude, and if applied at the wrong time they can actually increase the fluctuations. It is as hard for the government to anticipate the fluctuations as it is for speculators in the commodities markets who are trying to make money on them. Chronic instability could push economic activity down much faster than would otherwise be necessary.

Even if it were somehow possible to rapidly decentralize the economy and to absorb the unemployed in small-scale manufacturing, agriculture, or the production of raw materials, a huge construction job would still be required to provide even minimal housing and public services in the right locations. Perhaps houses could be physically moved o where hey are needed, but it is also hard to imagine now this task could be done at the rate required. It is easier to imagine the mining boom towns of the past, with tar-paper shacks, tents, mud or dust everywhere, and crude sanitation. If such shanty towns did develop, there would soon be a wall of opposition in front of urbanites trying to escape the declining prospects of

the largest cities. This is not a very attractive eventu-
ality.

There could also be a great deal of harm done to the
environment if unskilled, urban folk tried to move
toward self-sufficiency too quickly. If unsuitable land
were cultivated, erosion could reduce its potential for
more appropriate uses, such as grazing or forestry.
During the Depression, woods were cut indiscrimi-
nately in a desperate effort to generate income, even
though the market was flooded with lumber and
building activity was at a standstill. The same despera-
tion could lead to destructive uses of crop land, grazing
land, and other resources.

Because of the experience of the Depression and all
the attention the economy has received since then, we
have a few ideas about how the economy might behave
under conditions of severe scarcity. But these ideas are
largely conjectural; we have not had any actual experience. The Marxists have been saying for years that
capitalism would collapse if profits fell or investments
went sour. Perhaps it will; no one can say for sure. Our
knowledge of individual behavior is even sketchier
than our knowledge of economic behavior.

There is not too much point in dwelling on what we
cannot know. Yet it is important to realize that pitfalls
exist if for no other reason than to help weaken our
confidence in the notion of growth at any price. And
there is already opposition to the uncontrolled development of energy resources — opposition that should
make overshoot and collapse less likely. This is the

great contribution of environmentalists; they have delayed and often stopped altogether many undesirable projects, thereby initiating the transition to frugality before anyone was aware of what was happening.

The important task now is to try to see how this transition can be allowed to take place smoothly and perhaps even enjoyably.

Easing into Frugality: A Guide to Urbanites

The goal of most people is to minimize change. This is not surprising, given the disturbing nature of so many changes today. But what may be surprising is that such an orientation is not necessarily in conflict with the process of moving toward frugality. It is possible to ease toward frugality slowly, and with a minimum of change. The trick, as far as the individual is concerned, is to be in a good position to take advantage of opportunities as they evolve and to avoid the traps. The most dangerous thing to do is to rigidly resist all change. As for society, "business as usual" is the surest way to bring on a dangerous pace of change later.

To try to go "back to the land" and to be economically self-sufficient is not a realistic alternative for many people today. In many ways it is not appropriate. We are still at the peak of the urban, industrial economy, just the opposite end of the economic spectrum from a self-sufficient, agricultural economy. To try to abandon all that when the modern system still has so much power and momentum left in it is premature. Besides, when we reach equilibrium sometime in the distant future, it is unlikely that we will have nearly as large a percentage of our population in agriculture as did earlier traditional societies. With the scientific and technical understanding we have, agriculture will inevitably be more productive than in the past, even if we become totally dependent on renewable resources. This increased productivity will leave broad opportunities in cities and towns. A great movement back to the land is not only unnecessary but could even be undesirable if it contributes to instability. The charge against the doomsayers is well taken — they tend to cause people either to overreact or else to fear change so much that they rigidly resist it. Both are undesirable responses.

Indeed, easing into frugality today, even while we still live in cities, can leave us with plenty of time to enjoy the authentic pleasures available in our society. Some are unique to the affluent society — the education, the books, the good communications, the opportunity to travel, and the extraordinary experiences possible in our fluid, individualistic society. Others are more universal — family, friends, eating, drinking, working, playing in the park, or walking down the avenue. Whatever one's tastes, there are pleasures to be enjoyed and cultivated. There is no reason to abandon them.

This is not to suggest that we should behave as if

there were no tomorrow. Some sensible, modest steps should also be taken to protect one's future prospects, to avoid getting too far into a corner. The greatest concern will be for one's livelihood. If it looks as if higher prices for energy and raw materials will seriously weaken one's job, it would be a good idea to keep an eye out for a stronger industry to work in. Even this, however, is not absolutely essential; those who intensely enjoy their work are probably doing a good job and would be in a good position to survive a retrenchment. The auto industry will keep on producing cars under the worst of circumstances, even when cars become glorified bicycles on four wheels run by lawnmower motors. Others, who do not feel strongly about what they are doing, will be more apt to remain open to other opportunities. But the most foolish thing to do is to fight to hold on to an uninspiring job in a declining industry; this is simply defending one's place in the trap.

Another prudent step is to learn simple but useful skills around the house, the garage, and the garden. Learning how to work with your hands can be enjoyable. It can also be valuable when a personal financial squeeze develops (which for some people has already occurred). But the basic advantage of knowing how to do many things is that having a range of skills may be enormously valuable if one is laid off or if the economy moves in a more labor-intensive direction. It is, of course, hard to know what skills will make the difference; whatever is most pleasurable is as logical a choice

as any. But the feeling of being a little bit better prepared to cope with economic reversals can be a good
feeling. And one's self-confidence in the face of uncertainty is as effective a tool as any.

There are a number of other practical steps that will
not only improve one's ability to weather economic setbacks, but will also contribute to the easing of scarcity
as well. A number of these steps are obvious and are already being taken by some: buying a smaller car, insu-
lating the home, and generally reducing material consumption. A significant step in this respect would be to
move closer to work and shopping areas and reduce
dependence on the private car. From a conservation
point of view -- which will more and more be analogous to a dollars-and-cents point of view as energy gets
more expensive — the best place to live will be in an
area with high population density. High density has a
number of practical advantages: Town houses and
apartments insulate each other and tend to reduce energy demands; they consume less land; they can be
served efficiently by public transportation; shops and
services are usually nearby, often within walking distance; and the cost of maintaining streets and utilities
is substantially less because distances are shorter. On
top of these material advantages, there are social ones
as well. With a higher population density, there are
more things to do, more chances to run into friends in
shops or on sidewalks, and more opportunities for all
the truly urban experiences that Jane Jacobs describes
well in *The Death and Life of Great American Cities*.[1]

It is sad that there has been so much opposition to high density. This opposition has contributed to the rapid sprawl that is now so characteristic of modern cities. True, sprawl would have occurred anyway, without the opposition; the suburban house has been the preferred type of dwelling for a long time now, as evidenced by the high prices we are willing to pay for them. (Builders naturally respond by building suburban houses since they are profitable.) As resources get scarce, however, suburban areas will become more and more expensive to live in, and if discretionary use of the private car is restricted, they will become traps as well. The prudent thing is to anticipate this possibility and to relearn the urban pleasures we have largely forgotten during our sojourn in the suburbs. The hard part of all this is, of course, that the city centers are often old and run down. Yet, in many cities, restoration is going on, particularly by young people who cannot afford new homes in the suburbs. This is the economics of resource scarcity working as it should.

Several surveys have shown that many Americans would prefer to live in small towns or rural areas if they could. A 1972 Gallup survey found that only 13 percent of Americans prefer to live in cities, down from 22 percent in 1966, while 55 percent prefer small towns or rural areas.[2] I must admit to some skepticism about these figures; I cannot help feeling that we are more addicted to urban diversions than we realize. The real ideal, I suspect, is to live in a rural area within driving distance of urban amenities. But this is the ideal that created suburbia; the only trouble was that there was no way for the first suburbanites to keep others from following them into the countryside around cities. Soon, rural values were destroyed by more and more subdivisions, while the abandonment of the city centers deteriorated urban values as well.

Still, from a resource point of view, the tendency to move away from the largest urban areas is a sound one (providing it is not just a longer commute). Already, unemployment is highest in the largest urban areas, particularly the industrial ones, and the cost of living is going up rapidly. As resource scarcity takes its course, we are likely to see a new urban scene evolve, one in which regional cities and towns are more prominent than the largest urban areas which dominate the pattern of population distribution today. The tendency to move to a smaller city is a good one, for the individual as well as for the process of adapting to scarcity.

A consequence of frugal behavior today should be the accumulation of savings in one form or another, at least for those of us with decent jobs. And even though it sounds crass, money is freedom in this society. With savings, it is possible to change and adapt as may be necessary. Without savings, there is more of a chance of being trapped in an unfavorable situation. To "put something away for a rainy day" is still a prudent thing to do.

But frugality is not parsimony; there is no point in denying everything to prepare for a future we cannot know, just as it is foolhardy to live only for today and let the future take care of itself. Many of the surest pleasures are inexpensive. It is primarily ostentatious consumption, the trying to keep ahead of the Joneses, that is so expensive. A movement that tended to ignore what the Joneses had and replaced it with the cultivation of simple pleasures would undermine the economic pressures of our society. With the niche of industrial society filling up, this can be expected to happen; there will be fewer opportunities to make a fortune, just as the opportunities to secure what is currently considered a middle-class standard of living are being constricted. To carefully consider what is personally important and satisfying, in effect to "know thyself," would be a reasonable and deliberate step toward living successfully with scarcity.

Plunging into Frugality: Problems of Pioneering

It is sometimes suggested that if economic growth ended, it would mean the end of change; life would become repetitious and monotonous without the challenges and opportunities we have had in the past. This, of course, is virtually an impossibility. The challenges will be different, but we will not get away from change that easily, not for a long time, anyway. When a degree of stability is finally reached sometime in the obscure future, our descendants will probably be ready for it.

The word "adapt" comes directly from the Latin word *adaptare,* meaning to fit. To be well-adapted is to fit well into one's situation, to be at ease and relaxed, instead of restless and dissatisfied. We have all known well-adapted people at one time or another who are perfect for the time and place they are in — a great teacher or salesman, a grizzled old fisherman, or a tramp. It is an envious position to be in, to fit so well, but it can also be a hazardous position with the world changing as much as it is today. The great teacher may be forced to use new teaching techniques or textbooks; the salesman may be forced by a merger from a small personal operation to a large bureaucratic one; expensive modern fishing boats may destroy the livelihood of the old fisherman; and prosperity may reduce the fellowship of the open road.

It is the "maladapted" who have created the modern world. They were the ones eager to capitalize on the changes that were undermining the well-adapted. Certainly, our society seems to reflect the restlessness and the dissatisfaction of those who shaped it. The steady stream of efforts to improve things, both from the personal point of view and for society as a whole, must say something about our assessment of ourselves and our society. It will also be those who feel least comfortable with the competition, the impersonality, and the impermanence of the modern world who will be the pioneers in the movement toward a simpler way of life.

In our fluid society it is a normal thing for individuals to maintain a running comparison of their situation with alternatives that come to their attention. Everyone has some dissatisfactions that cause one's mind to wander down different roads to see where they go — to look around with the kind of eyes that put oneself into the picture seen, and to compare it with one's own situation. If the prospect pleases and seems possible, it generates excitement and anticipation. In this comparison, between the existing situation and an alternative, the pros and cons of the existing situation are normally well known — how secure the job is, how happy the family is, what friends one has, what pleasures can be enjoyed, and what torments and hostilities are to be endured. The alternatives are more questionable; this is where the risk comes in. Even if the present situation is barely tolerable, it is usually necessary to have a fairly well-defined alternative before an individual, and especially a family, can make a major change.

Most people investigating alternatives will run into barriers of one sort or another — inadequate capital, lack of economic potential, an awkward transition — or the alternatives may just not appear so attractive on close examination. But even if nothing comes of such investigations, just the consideration of an alternative will make it a little harder to go back to the old job, and the excitement and anticipation will remain.

Sometimes fortuitous circumstances make a change possible. Some "half-way house" may be found in which the alternative can be tried without cutting off the security of the old job completely, or friends may offer a cooperative arrangement that makes it easier for both parties as well as providing a degree of mutual support. Perhaps the risks will be reduced when the children's education is completed and they are off on their own. Or an inheritance may provide some capital. Even a setback can force a change — the loss of a job, a particularly disturbing crime nearby, or not getting admitted to graduate school. Or perhaps the impetus will just be the long-term trends — income falling behind prices, higher taxes, rising crime rates, or declining mobility. Whatever the trends may be, as the current situation declines, the choice will shift toward a major break with things as they are.

The most important obstacle to small-scale alternatives is the difficulty of finding a way to obtain a living. There will be only a limited number of new economic opportunities until prices for energy and raw materials go up substantially over present levels. In the meantime, the uncertainties are great. How much easier it would be if we knew for sure how fast the price of energy will go up, how the rising cost of transportation will affect population distribution, or how land prices will change. For example, it could be very advantageous to buy a small farm if the price of food went up in the future along with present increases in the prices of farm equipment, energy, and chemicals; such a combination would make a small, labor-intensive farm economically viable. But if a recession were to come along or agricultural surpluses reappeared, the same small farm might not produce enough income to make mortgage payments. Or again, a bakery in a small town requires customers to survive; if the town's population stagnated, a bakery might be a marginal operation, but if the population increased, the baker might congratulate himself or herself for getting in "on the ground floor."

In a sense, there is no point in struggling with these economic imponderables. The current market values for businesses and land are a broad composite assessment of their economic potential as judged by buyers and sellers, and it is pretty hard for anyone to claim better knowledge. Every investment has its risks, and whether the risks are worth undertaking depends primarily on the individual's assessment of how desirable his or her life will be as a result. People willingly accept a low income if they love the work and the way of life that goes with it.

Whether the alternatives are viable does not depend entirely on how much money can be made. More and more, the key to economic survival will be *to learn how to get by with less income*. There are many opportunities to make a modest income; they will become economically viable opportunities to the first people that are able to get by on the small income generated. It is frugality that has allowed the Briarpatch network, a group of small independent entrepreneurs doing what they want to do on reduced incomes, to flourish in the San Francisco Bay Area. It is also what has allowed the Amish to thrive and expand on small farms all during the period when most small farms were going out of existence. *A low income is the heart of frugality.*

It takes a highly motivated and creative person or family to undertake the risk of developing his own

work while getting by with less and learning how to become more self-sufficient. For the first pioneers, it can
be lonely and difficult work in unfamiliar territory.
The frequently heard criticism that says these people
are "dropouts," and that they do not contribute their
skills and energies to solving society's problems, is totally wrong. They are doing a task that is essential for
our future, developing new skills and ways of living
that will provide models for others as necessity pushes
more of us in that direction. Nothing could be more
important. The pioneers are opening up new economic
territory where subsequent settlers can join them.

Families are also more likely to pull together for
many of the same reasons mentioned earlier. Arrangements between family members do not entail such involved legal arrangements as between unrelated
parties, and the traditional separation of labor in a
family, where the older members help around the
home so that the younger generation can devote more
of their energy and attention to an economic enterprise, may again be of real assistance.

What is now being called the household economy, in
fact, may emerge as a key adaptive strategy between
easing into frugality and plunging in all the way.[3] The
logic of the household economy has its basis today in
the affluence of parents, who often have secure, well-
paying jobs and mortgage-free homes, at a time when
their sons or daughters cannot find work. These young
people could give up the discouraging task of searching
for a regular job if they could find some way to earn

money on their own. If they are living at home anyway, any work is better than none, and parents might be expected to help financially to get them started. There are many possibilities: taking care of lawns; repairing neighborhood cars, bicycles, or appliances; refinishing furniture; taking care of children for working parents; washing store windows; installing insulation or solar heaters; or restoring old houses. Several enterprises could be developed, or perhaps a part-time job could be a supplement — anything to make some money. This kind of work could enable the young person to gain valuable experience and, in time, to become fully independent. It would also reduce the feeling of being trapped by unemployment. And it involves the labor-intensive kind of activities appropriate for the future. It could lead, in time, to profitable businesses.

If unemployment rates continue to rise or incomes to fall, the family will undoubtedly become more significant as an economic unit than it is now. Especially if unemployment hits the breadwinner, everyone in the family will have to pitch in and help. Or, an extended family could sell their assets in a region with declining economic prospects, pool their capital, and use it to get started somewhere else where the prospects look better. This could be an excellent way of adapting to scarcity and would benefit the family at the same time.

Individual and family economic alternatives will develop as circumstances and individual ingenuity make them possible. That could take time. We could use more large-scale community alternatives right now, if for no other reason than to absorb unneeded labor. The commune movement was a discouraging one, on the whole. The best that can be said for it is that it demonstrated a good deal about what was practical and what was not. It showed, most significantly, that it is not possible to have the best of all possible worlds — combining togetherness, sharing, and simplicity with complete freedom in personal relationships and sexual matters, and asking for no sense of duty to stick out the hard times or to be on good terms with one's neighbors. That vision of the good life, in which there were to be huge benefits at practically no cost, has, at least for the time being, been put to rest.

The communes that survived, greatly reduced in number, have much more structure and usually have a religious basis. A notable one is The Farm, which was organized by Stephen Gaskin after he and a group of followers had left San Francisco in 1971 in a small fleet of old buses. They finally settled in Tennessee and purchased land in a thinly populated county, and now one thousand people of all ages (though mostly young) support themselves quite well on 1,700 acres of land. A dozen other Farms have been spawned elsewhere and together support another six hundred members. Besides farming, The Farm operates its own bank, construction company, private utilities, schools, and medical clinic, where the group delivers their own babies. They also ask pregnant women to come and have their babies there instead of having abortions and, if they wish, to leave the babies with The Farm as long as necessary. Membership in The Farm is only granted after a trial period, and it requires a vow of poverty and the turning of personal wealth over to the cooperative, so membership is not taken lightly. The Farm had enough surplus, after being in existence for only three years, to form an international aid service called Plenty, which provided substantial assistance to Guatemala after the earthquake of 1976.[4]

The main weaknesses of these "technicolor Amish," as they describe themselves, would seem to be their dependence on the charismatic religious leadership of Stephen Gaskin and the traditional difficulties of sustaining a communal way of life. Although aspects of many societies are run communally, complete communal societies are a very rare phenomenon in history, which suggests that they are difficult to sustain. The loss of a strong leader often leads to an organization's breakup, unless a sound operating structure has been built. A better basis than communes for decentralized groups would seem to be communities — for example, a community organized under the auspices of an established organization. A community based on a known organization, philosophy, religious faith would be more apt to receive financial support and local acceptance. Bureaucracy has its usefulness too. Established organizations could better assure the continuity of the community and would be more likely to attract members from all parts of society than just the affluent young, the main group involved with the communes. The Black Muslims and CORE, the Congress of Racial

Equality, have both developed cooperative economic activities in the south, since they concluded a long time ago that northern cities would never provide a good life for poor blacks. Cooperatives are also an attractive alternative to what is often experienced as the lonely and threatening world of commercial competition. Individuals with land or economic enterprises could work them cooperatively, if they felt strongly enough about the particular philosophical basis on which the cooperatives were organized.

Any alternatives that might evolve, whatever their form or function, will make a major contribution to the economy and to the choices available to people. If their numbers were to increase substantially, it is possible that the shortfall in jobs could be reduced, greatly easing the adjustment to scarcity. But whatever their numbers, successful communities will be valuable additions to the range of models available to others in the future. New communities may have to struggle for a long time before getting firmly established, but this should not be held against them; it is characteristic of the muddling process. Such tasks are not easy and straightforward.

The Politics of Decentralization

American society has always honored independence and the pioneer spirit. In general, it was not hostile to the utopian and socialistic experiments of the nineteenth century. Even the commune movement of the

1960s received quite a bit of approval from American idealists in the beginning. There is no reason to assume this general attitude will change, especially since the decentralized alternatives offer the promise of removing some of the overload from the economy and will enable the rest of society to go on with less unemployment and less scarcity. From now on, anybody who leaves a regular job for one that effectively removes him or her from the labor market will be doing society a favor. The kindest thing I could do for my unemployed colleagues with advanced degrees would be to quit my teaching job so one of them could have it. For this simple but basic reason, there is not likely to be any general opposition to decentralization, although there may be opposition to some of the specific consequences, especially in areas receiving an influx of outsiders. But to the degree that decentralization incorporates traditional American virtues it could be seen as the meritorious thing to do.

Because of these benefits, the government is not likely to hinder the movement to frugality. But could it do very much to encourage it? Not too much, as far as I can tell. Decentralization will occur primarily because of slowly intensifying scarcity, and the government is not likely to speed this up. One traditional function of government is to facilitate the flow of information and research, but this is already being done by the growing number of books and magazines that report the grassroots economic experiments going on in many parts of the country. If the government plays a role in the process of adjusting to scarcity, it will probably be in the area of reducing the financial risks of change.

The risk of failure will always act as a major inhibitor of change. It is a pretty gutsy thing to do what a lot of people would like to do — quit an unrewarding job, sell the house, and start out independently somewhere else. It is hard to give up security, even a rather unpleasant security, for something that is uncertain. The government could help here by putting a floor under the risk, so that bankruptcy and trying to get the old job back are not the specters that hang over every hopeful scheme. If our present welfare system were replaced by a single guaranteed income, it would act as such a floor. Then, if the first economic venture failed, or took longer to get started than expected, the guaranteed income would help one to weather the lean period.

A guaranteed income would have a number of advantages compared to present forms of unemployment and welfare programs.[5] A federal guaranteed income would provide uniform benefits nationwide, encouraging people to move to places where the cost of living is less, such as small towns and rural areas. Existing programs pay higher amounts in urban areas because the cost of living is higher there, but this encourages the poor to stay in the cities. Once drawn away from economically stressed urban areas by uniform benefits everywhere, people would be better situated to find day labor jobs, to learn new skills, to have a garden or cut firewood, and to take advantage of decentralized economic opportunities as they evolve.

One of the most disturbing visions of the future is that of a vast number of destitute people stuck in cities that increasingly assume the appearance of ghettos. Any program that tended to reduce that situation would be very valuable. Welfare cannot be eliminated since it sustains life in many parts of the inner city, but welfare could be modified in order to encourage a personal response that is more consistent with the long-run interests of the poor as well as the overall needs of society.

There is one more thing the government could do that would almost surely facilitate the response to scarcity, and that would be to loosen up the regulations that currently make unorthodox economic activity and housing so difficult. Zoning, labor restrictions, and building codes all had their logic at one time, usually to control rapacious factory owners, developers, and retailers who were trying to exploit their workers or the public — activities characteristic of the heyday of capitalism. These regulations will be less appropriate for the needs of a decentralizing economy. A number of these regulations could be dropped without difficulty, as time passes, while others could be modified. This process is sure to be slow and messy. Those who benefit from the regulations will try to maintain their advantage as long as they can. But an alliance between conservatives and liberals can already be seen forming in current deregulation cases. The conservatives, who are opposed to government regulation on principle, align themselves with liberals who are opposed to subsidizing powerful industries. This alliance seems certain to gain strength as the disadvantages of various regulations become more obvious. As these regulations are eroded, the process of decentralization should quicken.

The Need for Patience

If the pioneers do their work well — discovering or reviving new ways suitable for our transition to a frugal economy — and the rest of society eases in the same direction with prudence and, one hopes, good humor, the prospect of running out of energy will no longer generate the nightmares it now does. We will awake to find that the sun is rising on a modest way of life which affords us few illusions of grandeur, but permits the exercise of many human instincts often frustrated at present. Once the simple, decentralized way of life becomes discernable and is seen to be a good life, the evolution toward it could even get ahead of the rate of change forced by the shortage of resources. This may be too much to hope for, but if it did occur it would do wonders to ease up the tensions and frustrations that exist in our society now.

As hopes and aspirations shift toward a simpler way of life, there may be some impatience while the decentralized alternatives develop. I often find myself in this position. I tell myself how important it is that plenty of time be available to muddle toward frugality, but I still secretly cheer to myself when oil drilling on the continental shelf produces "dry" holes or the big new atomic power plants have operating troubles. I worry that things will move too slowly, and that I shall not live long enough to be a part of the work of rebuilding with family and friends, to enjoy hammering the boards of a close community with my neighbors, to pay tribute to the good earth, to watch my grandchildren grow up close at hand.

In my impatience, the trends seem to change almost imperceptibly. But the trends are there. Rural property values, after being depressed for years, are rising faster than urban property values, meaning that the demand is shifting in that direction. Labor-intensive industries are more profitable than capital-intensive ones. Urban unemployment rates are higher than rural rates. Incomes are now only fitfully keeping up with the cost of living. The Population Reference Bureau reports that the percentage of Americans that move each year is down slightly (although it is 17.7 percent). The Stanford Research Institute claims that *voluntary simplicity,* a personal economic decision, is growing very rapidly.[6] More and more people are making small-scale independent enterprises go.

We are experiencing the top of the curve of Figure 2 that was presented at the beginning of this chapter, a period of some ten to twenty years during which environmental resistance slowly brings growth to a standstill before contraction sets in. It is an ambiguous era because both optimists and pessimists can read the fluctuations as supporting their forecasts. Until the line heads downward irreversibly, the social ambivalence and contradictions will remain. But it looks as if things are on schedule. All it takes is patience.

CHAPTER VIII

The Pros and Cons
of Underdevelopment

Let us say that the argument of this book is correct, that the industrialized countries will be unable to transcend the approaching problems of resource depletion, that international trade will decline, and that we will be more and more absorbed by our own transition to a frugal way of life. What are the implications of this for the poor countries of the world, who are already struggling with great poverty and overpopulation? Would this not consign the underdeveloped countries to continued stagnation and the horrible prospect of overpopulation and eventual famines? Isn't it our help that provides the best hope for their development and a decent future?

These questions are by no means straightforward ones. For one thing, it is becoming increasingly difficult to envision how our assistance could actually help resolve the predicament of Third World countries. The conventional wisdom is familiar enough. Economic and technical aid is carefully applied in order to trigger an economic takeoff that eventually becomes self-sustaining. Education is encouraged to overcome ignorance and superstition, and together with health measures, it leads to a more productive work force. Then as modernization occurs birth rates fall, because there are more regular jobs, more women in the work force, and increased urbanization. This pattern of development is the one that has occurred in several countries that have made the economic takeoff successfully — Japan, Taiwan, Singapore, and Brazil — and it even reflects, to a degree, the process of our own development. It is an attractive vision for us, partly because it has parallels with our own heritage; imitation is the sincerest form of flattery.

But most countries are a long way from making this transition. Plagued by large, rapidly growing populations and very limited resources — cultural as well as natural — for modernization and economic development, they are failing to make the takeoff, and instead, they tend to sink farther into poverty. One factor alone makes the prospects for economic development almost impossible to visualize: There are simply not enough natural resources to support our form of abundance worldwide. If we in the developed countries are unable to sustain our resource use, what are the prospects for the billions of poor people who occupy so much more of the globe? Even if we shared all we have — which will not happen — it would not go very far, or last very long.

There is another factor that might be equally as intractable as natural resource limits and that is the cultural resources necessary for development. Many traditional societies are based on ethical systems that are very much opposed to the values of either the free market economy or socialism, the two models of development presently available to them. How could the traditional ways of so many people be changed quickly enough to do much good before current population increases lead to famine? Or, from another perspective, are we sure enough about what we have to offer other countries to justify breaking down cultural systems that have evolved over thousands of years? The worst outcome that can possibly be imagined would be the disappearance of traditional ways just as the resource underpinnings of a modern, industrialized way of life collapse, leaving the underdeveloped countries with nothing.

Without question, uncontrolled population growth is the great tragedy of the underdeveloped countries. It is forcing a painful deterioration in their ways of life and, at the same time, acting as a major barrier to economic development. In most underdeveloped countries the percentage of the population who are dependents — under fifteen years of age — ranges from 40 to 50 percent. Trying to provide so many youngsters with food, clothing, and education, and then a job, plus all the other things that must go with economic development — transportation systems, communication networks, financial services, and marketing organizations to distribute goods — is a superhuman task. In the developed world, it took several hundred years to build this infrastructure, during which time high-grade resources were available, wealth was pulled in from around the world, and population growth was much slower. Europe was also fortunate in being able to export its excess population, an opportunity not available to underdeveloped countries today. To believe, then, that a similar process of economic development can occur in the underdeveloped countries in the next several decades seems to require a blind faith in the ultimate success of modern society. The job is so overwhelming that, sadly, economic aid may in truth be only a salve to our conscience rather than a real help to others.

It may be a salve in another sense too. Our military grants exceed grants for economic aid, and both are given with many political strings attached. Private investments are designed primarily to produce a profit for investors; the consequences for the country involved, whether good or bad, are of secondary importance. So let us at least be honest with ourselves about the nature of our foreign aid; what we do for the underdeveloped countries, we do largely for our own purposes.

There is a general feeling that there must be something that we can do that is unequivocally good to help the less fortunate. But other than birth control measures, such contributions are hard to find. Health care is the classic example. We still hear stories that were common in the past of newly discovered peoples who seem happy and easygoing, and without all the pressures of modern society. The only defect in their way of life is the disease that is present and the high infant mortality rates. Health care seems to be the perfect area to offer help — to reduce suffering, debilitation, and the heartbreak of the death of a child. Just the diseases and infant mortality are to be attacked; everything else is to be left as it was. So the vaccinations, the insecticides, and the sanitation measures are brought in, and for a while things go well; life is better. But then other changes begin to occur as the population increases. Farming spreads to marginal lands, and erosion becomes a problem. Grazing land and firewood gets scarce. The landless and unemployed start to accumulate in the main towns looking for food and work. Efforts to provide jobs for them lead to additional immigration from the poverty-stricken rural areas, and shanty towns appear and with them all the urban ills. Discontent increases, a revolutionary movement develops, and pretty soon all the problems that plague poor countries are there. A way of life is overwhelmed and begins to disappear. The introduction of one outside activity, benevolent in itself, into a stable traditional system causes a disequilibrium that eventually undermines the entire society.

What leads people in less developed countries to have so many children? Are they so stupid or uneducated as to not see the ultimate outcome that is staring them in the face? Yet they could just as well ask us, "Are you so stupid as to go on using more and more nonrenewable resources when the ultimate outcome

stares you in the face?" The two questions are analogous. All people, whether from rich or poor countries,
must get by from day to day as best they can in the immediate situations they find themselves in. It is no help
for individuals to stand back and question things in
their society over which they have no control. In the
underdeveloped countries, children are an important
part of life, and they play an important economic role.
Their key asset is that they provide a form of social
security for their parents — to take care of them in
their old age and to surround them with grandchildren. The great fear is to be alone — to be without economic support and to be isolated from the fabric of
kinship. Until old age is reached, children help with
everyday tasks and cause little interference with the
parents' way of life since life centers in the village and
someone is usually around, an aunt or a neighbor, to
keep an eye on them. Children are a major source of
enjoyment in a simple society with few diversions. To
be sure that a son survived to take care of the parents
in their old age, it was traditionally necessary to have a
fairly large number of children. But today, because of
modern health measures, most children are surviving
— in contrast to the past — and the population explosion is the result.

People in the developed world are really no different; we are simply responding to another set of circumstances. Like everyone else we try to get by as best we
can. One has to find a job; find a place to live; purchase goods from those offered for sale; and find enjoy-

ments from those available in a highly mobile mass society. Young people have to get an education so they
will find good niches for themselves in the world. If a
conservation teacher were able to convince students to
behave in an ecologically rational way and use only renewable resources, that teacher would have prepared
his students for a way of life that hardly exists in this
country today. Societies are all of a piece; they are systems with their own internal logic and structure. It is
hard to mix one with another.

Besides population growth, there are many other examples of the unfortunate consequences that have followed the introduction of modern ways into underdeveloped countries, even when done with the best of mo-
tives. Weapons made life easier for hunters, but the
weapons also enabled the same hunters to overexploit
the animals in their environment. The importation of
inexpensive machine-made cloth and metalware displaced local craftsmen. Tractors displaced farm laborers, while enriching large landowners. The skills of
foreigners and the power of their machines have
tended to erode confidence in traditional sources of
authority and indigenous ways of doing things. And in
addition to the well-intended efforts to help the underdeveloped countries, there have also been the malevo-
lent ones: the slavery, the removal of precious metals
and art treasures, the exploitation of cheap labor, the
expropriation of raw materials, the setting up of puppet regimes and the sale of arms and expensive consumer goods to them. All of these things have occurred,

and, in many cases, the traditional ways of life have
weakened and broken. The result: in addition to being
as poor materially as they were before, such people
have become culturally impoverished as well. If culture is the most important possession that poor people
have because it helps make their life livable, its loss can
be a devastating blow. Poverty is one thing; people
can be happy and poor. But to be cut off from one's
way of life can produce the empty-eyed people seen in
the slums of cities all around the world.

Ruth Benedict recorded the way a Digger Indian in
California expressed his loss:

*'In the beginning,' he said, 'God gave to every peo-
ple a cup, a cup of clay, and from this cup they drank
their life. . . . They all dipped in the water,' he continued, 'but their cups were different. Our cup is broken
now. It has passed away.'*[1]

Under the impact of alien ways, the American Indians were left with no choice but to try to use the cup
offered to them; but it was offered only halfheartedly,
and the Indians were not comfortable using it since it
was such a different type of cup. It was said that the
Indians could have the best of both worlds, the best
from their own past and from our society; but cultures
cannot be mixed and matched that way. The Indian
remains a tragic figure who often falls between both
worlds, the old ways gone but not fitting into the new.
It is a sad story, the change from the proud, admirable
human beings recorded in books such as Theodora
Kroeber's *Ishi in Two Worlds* to the group in our so-

ciety with the highest incidence of alcoholism, illiteracy, mortality, and suicide.

It is done; all of this is behind us. What can be done now? Is there anything that we can do to ease the plight of the people who are still trying to cope with the spread of the same cultural force worldwide? The answer may be no.

How Population Growth in the Underdeveloped Countries Will End

Ever since farming began some ten thousand years ago, agricultural societies have encouraged large families. Agricultural societies were capable of supporting far larger populations than hunting and gathering societies. And there were also many benefits from a larger population. More people meant more social contact, greater cultural richness, and the benefits that came from the specialization of labor. The old chronicles of travelers speak of cultures with large populations in terms of wealth and advancement, while the thinly populated, remote regions were considered poor and backward. So it is not surprising that a pronatalist orientation became characteristic of agricultural societies, especially while the niche of agricultural society had so much space available. Even with such favorable conditions, population growth was slow because of high death rates.

But that is not the case today, and as population growth in traditional agricultural societies reaches its limits, it can be expected that the cultural values that favor large families will slowly be forced to give way. As with unwanted change in our own society, this might not happen until events bring it about. In the underdeveloped countries, this would mean all the things no one likes to think about: famine, disease, and epidemics. Famines make the headlines, following periods of bad weather or poor harvests; but general malnutrition will probably be the greater cause of suffering since it leaves people debilitated and without effective resistance to disease. The study of world population trends up to 1975 by the Worldwatch Institute reports a slight increase in death rates in several countries, a significant change from the long era of falling death rates in the underdeveloped countries.[2] The sad thing about famine relief, as it is practiced today, is that just enough aid is given to allow the stricken population to survive, but it leaves people in the same desperate situation as before, on the edge of survival with no margin of protection against the next lean time and no cultural shock strong enough to force a change in values about family size.

As heartless as it may sound, the merciful thing may be for some catastrophe to come quickly in the half dozen or so countries that are hopelessly overpopulated, a catastrophe that will drop population below where it is at present, ease the pressure on the surviving population, and provide undeniable evidence to encourage changed attitudes toward large families. Even that might not be adequate, and it could take several generations of unremitting population pressure before the necessity of population control is integrated into the culture. But at some stage the realization that family size must be limited will occur, and at that time current birth control efforts will pay off. The birth control devices already made available will be adopted rapidly; the cajoling and incentives now being used will no longer be necessary.

Is there any evidence that values as deep-seated and long held as those that favor large families can be changed by the force of such events? Yes, in the perspective of cultural evolution, there is such evidence. Hunters and gatherers must have gone through such a process after they first occupied the farthest reaches of the earth, and migration was no longer possible as a way to cope with overpopulation. When explorers and missionaries first observed tribal groups, they found that population levels were well below the maximum that could be supported with a hunting and gathering economy. At first this was interpreted simply as the result of primitive health care and a high death rate, but later, when anthropologists studied these groups more carefully, it was found that population control measures were being applied extensively from within the culture. The goal was to keep the population well below the carrying capacity of the environment; this was understood as essential for the good life. It meant that hunters and gatherers could eat the foods they preferred and could easily obtain, and could pass by the "starvation foods" that were eaten only when there was no other choice. With population control, hunters and gatherers had leisure, were well fed, and had a buffer against hard times.

The birth control measures they employed were unpleasant for the most part, often highly so.[3] There were many taboos on sexual intercourse that increased abstinence, and in some cases, crude methods of contraception and abortion were employed. Bride prices delayed marriage, and if times were difficult, the ordeals required of young men were increased in severity. If everything else failed, infants and old people were put to death. In almost all hunting and gathering societies, twins were considered unlucky, and one was put to death, usually by exposure. Among the Eskimos, old people voluntarily ended their lives when the group's survival was at stake — and it was not necessarily an unhappy event, this passage onto the next world after the best years in this life were over.[4] Certainly, none of these measures would have been introduced unless they were absolutely essential. But hunters and gatherers had plenty of time to learn; it took hundreds of thousands of years for human society to develop, and they learned that they had to give up the luxury of freely propagating children in return for the more important goal of a population in comfortable equilibrium with the environment.

Agriculturalists are approaching the same type of ecological situation regarding population and resources that hunters and gatherers surmounted. It is hard to say how long it will take agriculturalists to learn the same lesson. Fortunately, the unpleasant population control methods of the past are no longer necessary, but still it is hard to predict what will cause the ideas and techniques of modern birth control methods to be widely accepted. It may even be that population stabilization will be achieved with high birth rates and high death rates. Such a solution is not all bad; the continued presence of death may cause every day of life to be more appreciated, and it would at least produce a society rich in children, in contrast to the situation we ourselves will soon be facing, of a society dominated by old people, when birth rates are low and life spans are long. But high death rates would suggest that the ecological niche is crowded, and this means a marginal existence with strenuous efforts to survive, poor nutrition, and recurrent waves of acute suffering. The good life comes with a population well below the maximum possible.

It is painful to think of the cultural evolution that overpopulated countries still must face, but its ultimate value should not be forgotten. Robinson Jeffers points out that

What but the wolf's tooth whittled so fine
the fleet limbs of the antelope?[5]

The wolf's tooth of overpopulation will carve the final part of the cultural achievement of traditional societies — the ability to maintain populations well below the carrying capacity of the environment to assure a good life. It will put traditional society on a far sounder basis than its present incomplete evolution leaves it.

The result to be hoped for, a good and satisfying way of life that is intricately balanced with the environment, is a very beautiful thing. It is the kind of achievement that mankind should be proud of, one that benefits a whole people and the generations that follow. It is a more valuable achievement than the youthful successes of the modern world that so often honors achievement for achievement's sake, ignoring the consequences for the common good.

Although many traditional ways of life have disappeared under the onrush of change, a good many are resilient and are surviving, enduring difficult times with patience and fortitude. As the promises of modernization fade — promises that traditional societies were always skeptical of anyway — the tested ways of the past will regain their power to organize society. The old ways will endure, but not without changes, many of them beneficial. Let us hope that the cultural losses will not be too great.

Some Assets of Underdeveloped Countries

In this country there is a tendency to pity the people of the Third World, or to feel guilty about them, or to treat them with contempt. None of these attitudes is deserved. If we can exclude from our minds for a minute the staggering problem of overpopulation and the disequilibrium that goes with it, it can be seen that the underdeveloped countries have some considerable assets, three of which seem especially valuable.

(1) They rely upon local renewable resources. If our goal is to gain the security of relying on renewable resources, the underdeveloped countries are much closer to this goal than we are. The poorer and more "backward" a country is, the more likely it is to survive an energy shortage without painful readjustments; life will go on as it always has. The closer the people are to a subsistence economy, the less they will have to worry about factors beyond their control. The subsistence villager is free from the fears of falling prices for cash exports, higher prices for imported materials, boycotts, strikes by truck drivers, and unscrupulous middlemen. He has not become addicted to the things that can be purchased only with cash. If the villager is poor, the government will have less interest in him as a source of tax revenue. Village dwellings are simple structures built of local materials, such as clay, wood, or thatch. The community as a whole regulates water supplies, its own administration, the use of common lands, and religious functions. There is no reason why such a way of life could not continue indefinitely.

(2) They are well adapted to the environment. The fact that traditional societies have survived, often for thousands of years, is a good measure of proof that they have been good conservationists. If over the ages they had caused even some modest deterioration in the productivity of the environment, their sustenance would have been eroded eventually, and even destroyed. This surely must have happened to many groups, the ones we know of only by their archeological

remains. Yet, at the dawn of the modern era, there was still a vast array of groups with economies meticulously crafted to diverse soils, topography, vegetation, and climates. In many cases no other ways have been found to utilize environments such as tundra, semidesert, and tropical forests other than by traditional methods of herding or shifting agriculture. Sadly, a good number of these societies have been disrupted, a staggering cultural loss. It would have been good if some of the effort that has gone into preserving threatened species of wildlife had gone into preserving threatened ways of life as well. But many groups still survive; they range from the descendants of great civilizations to the remnants of minor tribes adapted to unique environments. These are the peoples that we, in our ethnocentrism, refer to as "underdeveloped." Their traditional methods of managing resources should not be allowed to die. To record them would be a more worthwhile form of research than that currently devoted to learning how to remove traditional obstacles to modernization.

(3) They are small in scale and decentralized. The village is characteristic of traditional societies, just as the city is characteristic of industrial society. The village constricts horizons and mobility, there is no question of that. But there are advantages as well in the greater depth of contact possible in a limited social and physical environment — its greater stability and the greater cultural unity it permits. The villagers know their small world intimately — its rhythms, its moods, its natural history, and all its human occu-

pants. The peasant works on the land or at a trade that his father and grandfather did before him; roots have not been allowed to wither, or ties to fragment. The beauty to be perceived in the village world is of the changing seasons, the ripening crops, children playing, and a mother nursing her infant. Peasants have not seen the art of all ages, as we have, but their own folk art grew out of their own experience and is an intrinsic part of it. Pervading everything are religious beliefs that give meaning to their lives, from the great events of birth, marriage, and death to the small objects that have been made sacred. The villagers do not question what is right or wrong; there is only one way, the way of their ancestors that has withstood the tests of time.

Nothing is all good or all bad; traditional societies have many disadvantages too. But as we find it harder and harder to resolve our own dilemmas we may begin to see the logic of traditional systems with new eyes. We will have to give up comfortable prejudices about our obvious superiority and start to look at traditional cultures as having some use to us.

Two Questionable Gifts: Trade and Education

Trade and education are two activities that play very important roles in our hopes for less developed countries; trade to bring in the goods necessary to provide better diets, medical care, and stronger economies; and education to create the skills necessary for the

transformation of society. But both present dilemmas;
whether they turn out to be helpful or not in the end
will depend on the directions traditional societies ultimately take. If they do achieve a substantial degree of
progressive change, trade and Western forms of education will have been an essential part of the process; but
if modernization is to fail, trade and education will
only speed the erosion of traditional ways and self-sufficient economies.

In 1960, I walked through the streets of Delhi with
an Indian friend who had just received an advanced
degree from the London School of Economics. As a
foreigner, I found it fascinating; the streets were
pulsing with life, with a great diversity of people, of
tasks being done, and of goods being sold. I was a bit
surprised to find that my Indian friend was somewhat
embarrassed by it all; to him, this street scene reflected
his country's backwardness rather than its colorful rich
heritage. My own feelings and observations were undoubtedly superficial, those of a tourist, but it still
seemed a shame that the educated elite, who are so influential in the governments of developing countries,
are often condescending to those whom they are supposed to be helping. This occurs whether the political
orientation of the elite is to the left or the right. Sometimes it seems that the left is even more ready to ram
unpopular programs through; the "revolution" has
been used to justify the most brutal activities.

It is little wonder that villagers are skeptical of governmental representatives who come to them with

alien ideas. Not trusting the government to have their best interests in mind, the safest thing for the villagers to do is to resist change. A fascinating account of the dynamics of this process is given in a paper entitled, "The Peasant View of the Bad Life," by F. A. Bailey, in which the government is seen as outside the moral community of the village — as the enemy bent on taking what is left of the valued things the peasants still have.

Beyond this category are people whose culture — the way they speak, the way they dress, their deportment, the things they speak about as valuable and important — places them unambiguously beyond the moral community of the peasant; revenue inspectors, policemen, development officers, health inspectors, veterinary officials and so on; men in bush shirts and trousers, men who are either arrogant and distant or who exhibit a camaraderie which, if the villager reciprocates, is immediately switched off; men who come on bicycles and in jeeps, but never on their feet. These are the people to be outwitted: these are the people whose apparent gifts are by definition the bait for some hidden trap.[6]

In underdeveloped countries today, the Western-educated elite has, in a very real sense, a personal stake in modernization. The knowledge and abilities they have are the product of another way of life, and it is only if the traditional world passes away that they will be able to play an important and prestigious role in society. It is not surprising that the educated elite have

little sympathy for traditional ways and are impatient
with farmers who refuse to switch from subsistence
crops to cash crops; who are reluctant to risk investments in chemical fertilizers and new high-yielding
grains; who refuse to work harder in response to economic incentives; and who continue to have large
families. All of these decisions by villagers tend to reduce the prospects for modernization. If developing
countries are to obtain the symbols of modernization
— the steel mills, the nuclear power plants, the jet
aircraft — and pay for them by exporting goods rather
than through foreign aid, then somehow commodities
must be produced that can be sold for cash in world
markets. All manner of coercion is utilized to achieve
this: taxes, government monopolies, and import tar-
iffs. In effect, peasants are forced to work for national
status symbols in which they have no interest.

An Indian economist, Kusum Nair, traveled extensively through India trying to find out why Western
models of economic development seemed to work so
poorly. The account of her experiences, in a book entitled *Blossoms in the Dust,* points out the frequency
with which education in the villages is not producing
the desired effect.[7] Instead of being of value in dealing
with village needs, education often leads young people
to believe that they are a superior class. They refuse to work with their hands, and instead demand
that the government provide jobs appropriate to their
education; the focus is on a job with the government.
(Anyone who has ever been to India knows about its

bureaucracy, which is everywhere, and everywhere a source of maddening frustration.) It is unfortunate that education does not lead to increased productivity, but to me the saddest part of Kusum Nair's account is that these educated young people will look down on their parents, even though the education was often provided at great sacrifice by the parents. Such educated offspring sometimes demand money for proper clothes and for coffee in the cafes. Perhaps the story will not be lost on other families who were considering trying to educate a son or daughter.

Traditional societies have always seen to it that the education necessary for their ways of life was provided. As in any society, education is essential if a way of life is to be passed on from one generation to another. In less developed countries, education is usually done by parents, relatives, village elders, and priests, plus regular teachers in some cases. Only certain groups regularly have learned to read and write, skills necessary for their role in the society; the oral tradition was the general rule. Because change was slow, if at all, there was no problem with the generation gap. But it is not correct to assume, because illiteracy is high, that education is necessarily lacking in such cases. Much more must be known before the adequacy of education can be assessed.

Trade is perhaps a more painful issue to consider since it can be a matter of life and death. To varying degrees, most countries are now dependent on trade to obtain things they cannot produce themselves; they do this by exporting goods to obtain the necessary cash. The mutual benefits flowing from trade are a major factor contributing to the peaceful — if not contented — relations between countries since there are few countries that could cope easily with an interruption of trade.

But for the purposes of reaching equilibrium (in the developed countries as well as the underdeveloped countries), trade encourages all the wrong trends. Imported food permits poor countries to get farther out on the limb of overpopulation and dependency, a limb that could break for any number of reasons: international financial difficulties, military conflict, worldwide food deficits, and eventually an energy crunch. This is the "utterly dismal" theorem that Kenneth Boulding warns against — that every life saved today without changing underlying trends simply means a larger population to suffer the inevitable disaster later on. If food can be imported, then a country is not so apt to focus attention on agriculture and birth control, and encourages the illusion that industrialization is the way to development. Trade causes attention to be directed toward what can be sold profitably on the world markets rather than toward the careful adjustment to local resources that contributes to long-run stability.

Trade contributes to disequilibrium in the developed countries as well. Trade permits us to continue the process of economic growth using the resources that can be gleaned from around the world as domestic resources are depleted. We get ourselves farther out on the limb of dependency, too, on imported raw materials. As imports increase, the task of balancing them with exports gets tougher and will continue to get tougher as more and more countries compete for the declining markets for manufactured goods. Sooner or later, we will be forced back on our own resources. In the meantime, the inevitable adjustments are delayed, and imported resources allow us to get farther away from anything that could be considered a sustainable way of life.

There are many hazards in a highly integrated world system of exchange. Not only could it be interrupted at any time, but more fundamentally, the extension of world trade goes against the ecological requirement for diversity. As more and more countries trust their prospects to expanded trade in order to get by from one year to the next, the whole system becomes more vulnerable; the scope of the dislocation, if it came, would be worldwide.

But there are hazards in everything we do; dependence on trade is just another element in a basically dangerous and unstable situation. As long as the system holds together, trade will delay the onset of population stability and the husbandry of resources. But it will not solve these problems, only create new dilemmas as time passes. For example, food-exporting countries, such as the United States and Canada, will have to decide what to do about a growing number of countries that need food but have no money or credit to pay for it. Industrialized countries, in Japan and some in

Europe, will find it harder to export the manufactured goods necessary to pay for increasingly expensive
imports of energy and other raw materials. At the
same time, there is likely to be a glut of unused industrial capacity as the demand for manufactured goods
weakens. The terms of trade of industrial countries are
likely to deteriorate; they will have to sell cheap and
buy dear. Countries farthest from an equilibrium between resources and population, whether developed or
underdeveloped, will feel the squeeze the hardest.
Egypt and Bangladesh will be in company with
England and Japan. The money from the oil-exporting
countries and the food-exporting countries will keep
world trade going for a while, but after a while they
will be trading with themselves as other countries are
slowly squeezed out of world markets and forced to go
it alone because of accumulated debt.

It is unlikely that any countries will voluntarily take
steps to discourage trade and start the adjustment to
equilibrium before it is forced on them. It is just too
painful a thing to do. Instead, they will waste a lot of
money and effort trying to expand trade. This may
make a difference in the short run; but the end result is
likely to be the one they have tried so hard to avoid —
the slow decline in trade and the increased reliance on
their own resources. It is the same pattern: the events
and the workings of things force what is in the best
interest of each country in the long run, but cause
short-term distress. No country can say that it is the
master of its own fate.

The End of Cultural Imperialism

Cultural imperialism is a strong term, yet the practice exists in many forms. It is the multinational firms who claim they are in business to provide jobs and increase the GNP of less developed countries. It is the Marxist revolutionaries who promise that with the overthrow of existing authority will come peace, prosperity, and brotherhood. It is the foreign governments that support puppet regimes with military aid. But, more than anything else, cultural imperialism has caused the population explosion.

It is not possible to put ourselves in the position of people who were born into very different circumstances. We cannot know how their minds work, or what would make them happy or cause them bitterness or despair; nor do we have the right to make decisions for them. We have not been very successful in helping our own minorities. Is there any evidence that we can do better with billions of the world's poor? In the past, when we had more confidence that we were on an upward step on the evolutionary ladder, we had less compunction about bestowing our benefits on other peoples, even if by force; it was the white man's burden to do so. Now, the disequilibrium has been triggered, and events are taking their course. But it is the thoughtless and often self-serving introduction of modern ways that caused the disequilibrium that should grieve us now, rather than the fact that we cannot do more about the final outcome.

Nor should we forget the substantial advantages the underdeveloped countries have, advantages that give them good, long-term prospects, even if in the near future they must face the ominous and staggering task of learning how to stabilize their populations at sustainable levels. In essence, there is only one major change required of them — population control — and it is possible that that could be accomplished relatively quickly. We, on the other hand, have a very long task ahead of us; a whole way of life must change. Even though we should have enough time to complete it without going through the fire the underdeveloped countries may have to experience, we still have a very long way to go to reach a sustainable way of life based on renewable resources. The world we have built is grossly unsuited to reliance on renewable resources or frugal ways. It is a long way home; we face the task of discovering and building a way of life that functions in equilibrium with the environment. At some stage, we are likely to look to less developed countries for ideas.

CHAPTER IX

Out of the Corner

It is understandable that a growing element of pessimism should have entered into our view of the future. After a long period of confident expansion — an expansion that we came to assume was the order of things — we are now starting to come up against barriers. As we explore these barriers we discover that they are stronger than we expected and that, in come cases, they actually appear to be pressing in on us. We seem to be working ourselves into a corner. The hoped-for technological breakthroughs to unlock the passage through these barriers have not appeared. Traditional liberalism and conservatism, both of which claim credit for the era of expansion, now seem equally unable to resolve the difficulties facing us.

But whether or not we are trapped in a corner depends on which way we are looking. To see only a corner is to look in only one direction. It is by refusing to turn away from the barriers directly ahead of us that the corner assumes the nature of an unresolvable problem, a trap. At some point, there will be no other choice than to look in another direction. The effort to push back the obstacles that form the corner will have become futile. There are constraints on the choices we have for providing basic human needs, of course, but to acknowledge constraints should not mean to ignore the real choices that are available.

In the past, we have been able to push aside everything that stood in our way. After each successive effort, the subsequent push has required more force. Now we are at the stage where we cannot muster the tremendous power needed to continue the process. In some ways, we are not even able to hold on to what we have gained. As a society, we might prefer to keep things the way they are now, but as time passes, this will not be an alternative. As the frontier era of the nineteenth century passed, so will the affluent era of the twentieth. We will have less and less choice but to turn toward frugality.

The Futility of Resistance

I am regularly surprised by the frequency of one specific response to the prospect of moving toward frugality. Many people freely express their own willingness to move toward a simpler way of life, but they do not believe others will do so. It is almost as if everyone else will somehow be immune to the pressures scarcity generates. The wealthy will somehow be able to hold on to their wealth and their position; the middle class will not accept a reduction in their affluence and easy life;

the poor will not forego their chance to have what others now have. Government will somehow be able to keep taxes high no matter how much the economy declines; and labor unions will continue to jack wages up no matter how much unemployment there is, while corporations will continue to pull strings worldwide and maintain profits even if trade drops off. Perhaps this expectation is the basis for pessimism about the future; without economic change there would be little basis for personal change, and there would indeed be grounds for pessimism about the adjustment to scarcity.

Other powerful civilizations at their peaks must have seemed equally resistant to change, even more so. In the fourth century, Rome exercised complete control over most of western Europe; what could bring it down? In the fourteenth century, the long stability of medieval Europe must have seemed as if it would go on forever. The landed aristocracy in eighteenth-century England seemed unassailable since they controlled so much land, the major source of wealth. Yet all were severely weakened within a century. Nothing is immutable.

The only real question, as far as I am able to discern, is not whether we will move toward frugality, but whether we will move to it efficiently and peacefully. Violence will always be a possibility. But violence is a risky business; the consequences of failure for those undertaking it must be compared with the difficulties of adjusting to frugality, in the same way that the possible benefits (and risks) of a nuclear attack by the United

States or Russia must be compared with the difficulties of continually living with an adversary armed with nuclear weapons. With resources, however, even if violence were somehow successful, it still would not bring back the era of resource abundance. From a number of points of view, violence is unlikely to be worth the risks involved.

We are more likely to create problems for ourselves by trying too hard to overcome the barriers directly ahead of us. We may well employ the breeder reactor, dam the last free-flowing streams, cultivate the last soils, and exploit the last resources, simply because change is so threatening. There may well be more government action to ensure that we all pull together, more profits to motivate industry to undertake bad investments, and less that is natural, less that is beautiful. It is not an attractive vision, doubly so, since it is not likely to work anyway. Higher prices, unemployment, inflation, and the prospect of greater social control and political conflict will slowly cause us to turn away from such effort.

The old order will try to urge us on; its leaders have a heavy personal investment in things as they are, in experience, education, and income. They will say that to turn away from the effort is to retreat from the qualities that made this country great. But the conditions that created this country were rare and unique — a wide-open continent and new technologies to exploit its resources. These conditions will not return; there is no way to recreate the frontier. The Industrial Revolution is ending, but we are left with its machinery. If our society is not to remain "an immense stamping press for the careless production of underdeveloped and malformed human beings," in Robert Heilbroner's phrase, it will be because individuals have abandoned their stations at the machines.[1] The old order will become increasingly isolated.

As time passes and the age of expansion is clearly seen to be over, the social values it fostered will lose their power and usefulness. When opportunities abounded, it made sense to give up longstanding ties to family, friends, and community for something better elsewhere; those who stayed behind became lost in obscurity. With the economic stakes so high, it became worthwhile to put every last ounce of competitiveness into the process. With large-scale enterprise and rapid mobility came the anonymity that hid the shoddy producer, the exploiter, the huckster, even the criminal; with no effective community to resist, government had to be expanded to protect society. Individuals were left with little choice but to venture into the large-scale market economy and to try to achieve wealth and position, the primary measures of individual worth in such a society.

But as resources grow scarce, mobility declines, and decentralization occurs, all of this will slowly change. A new social logic will assert itself. Fewer resources will mean that sharing and cooperation will be functional if the frugal life is to be a good and full one. With less mobility and closer communities, it will not be necessary to rely on government so much for protection. For a person to live in a small community with the reputation of being a miser, a cheat, a spreader of malicious rumors, or a thief is strong persuasion against such behavior. Loyalty, trustworthiness, generosity, and goodheartedness are more apt to be virtues by which an individual is known, and one's good name will be important for full participation in the community. There will be fewer opportunities for the exploitive self-centeredness so characteristic of present society now. *Individual responsibility will be in one's own self-interest.* "As you sow, so shall you reap" will once again have real meaning. Those who contribute most to the enjoyment of life will be the most honored, rather than those who can take the most. Labor will once again be an act of love, for family, friends, and community.

Traditions are simply devices that evolve over long periods of time to make life richer and more satisfying. In a sense, they are contrived devices to get people to do what is in their own best interests as well as in the best interests of their community. All societies have them; it is only our obsessive individualism that has come to deny the validity of traditions, to say that they interfere with an individual's full development. In fact, the effect of traditional systems of conduct is just the opposite; they provide a stable framework for individual fulfillment. In traditional societies, the age-old question of whether people are basically good or evil is answered very simply; all individuals are assumed to have tendencies toward doing good and doing ill. Societies strive to encourage the good and restrain the bad through the establishment of acceptable modes of behavior — through traditions.

Because our heritage is so diverse, we have an unusually large reservoir of these products of cultural evolution to draw on as our own cultural evolution takes place. Our own heritage is our greatest resource, and the exotic imported philosophies that interest us now are likely to turn out to be more a reflection of our alienation than anything else.

Our social and ecological situation is a new one, and so it is inevitable that the future will bring with it new ways of thinking and acting. But if history can be used as a guide, it is likely that the most important social advances will come from the revitalization of elements from our own past that have been lost under the force of events. The stage would seem to be set for such an advance at this time.

Things Fall Together

Yeats's poem, "The Second Coming" contains the well-known line:

Things fall apart; the center cannot hold.

From the narrow perspective of urban, industrial society, this line may be appropriate, but this by no means leads inevitably to the dominant theme of the poem:

Mere anarchy is loosed upon the world,
The blood-dimmed tide is loosed, and everywhere

The ceremony of innocence is drowned;
The best lack all conviction, while the worst
Are full of passionate intensity. [2]

Perhaps anarchy would be the result if we played out
the role of the tragic hero trying to overcome the
greater and greater obstacles directly ahead of us. Fortunately, however, most of us are more flexible than
that; we watch for things that are best for ourselves
and our families. As the center fails, the result will not
be collapse; the edges will swirl into eddies that form
new centers. This process has already begun.

The end of an era is approaching — not the end of
the world. From the vantage point of the future, the
era of resource abundance will very likely be seen as an
aberration, as an abnormality, in the long stream of
human life. It will be seen as an extraordinary period,
no doubt, but one that was very hard on people pre-
cisely because of its great achievements which caused
so much disequilibrium. At least it is running its
course. Hopefully we will be spared the abrupt disloca-
tions brought about by conquerors or civil war. We
should also be able to avoid the fate of other powerful
cultures — the senility and decadence that lingers on
when power outlives the creative forces that built the
culture originally. Resource scarcity should accomplish that for us.

We are entering the future with a great deal in our
favor. We have peace, a vast storehouse of knowledge,
plenty of the necessary resources of land, water, air,

and sunshine, the tools we need, the scientific knowledge of how to use them effectively, and a rich cultural heritage to draw on. We have enough time to learn how to do things with our own hands once again, how to pull communities back together, how to raise our children, and how to allow our elders a useful and agreeable life. Although some of the changes will be awkward, many others will be challenging and fulfilling, and everywhere there will be opportunities for healthy work, new ties with family and friends, and activities to bring us closer to nature. If we do not succeed in making the adjustment, we will have no one to blame but ourselves.

Above all, it can be a good life. In effect, we will be exchanging the grand achievements of large-scale technological society for modest accomplishments on a more human scale. We will once again be a part of mankind's great journey, no longer set apart from it and seeking to manipulate it like technological gods. We will regain a degree of stability that will permit the deepening of culture and the enrichment of lives lived simply. Above all, we will have the comfort of knowing that our relationship with the environment is sustainable, and that the earth is a true home to us.

Acknowledgments

I have no way to trace all my debts in order to acknowledge them. All I can do is to thank those who have stimulated me most over the years: Kenneth Boulding, Garrett Hardin, E. F. Schumacher, Robert Heilbroner, Harrison Brown, Richard Wilkinson, Joseph Meeker, Karl Polanyi, Jane Jacobs, Marshall Sahlins, Robinson Jeffers, Henry Thoreau, Geoffrey Chaucer, and the anonymous authors of the Bible and other sources of ancient wisdom. The list goes on; my debts are great. I hope any injustices that I have done will be forgiven.

A number of people have been of real practical help to me on this project, mainly my wife Martha, who tells me when I am straying too far from the track, Loren Fisher for his encouragement, especially in the early stages when it was so important, James Robertson for his editorial advice, and Gwen Gardner and Bill Crutcher for their expert typing. I would also like to express my appreciation to colleagues who have read and commented on the manuscript: Gary Suttle, Burr

Keen, Ned Greenwood, Herbert Woodward, Don Bridenstine, Carl Emerich, George Cox, and Charles Cooper.

If I look at the world and see things differently, it is because of a fortunate combination of circumstances. I have chanced upon interesting work and opportunities to travel in these stimulating, if daunting, times. My parents gave me all the support anyone could wish for while still encouraging me to be independent. I consider myself well blessed with a good wife and two fine sons. I have benefited from good teachers, friends, colleagues, and inquiring students. All of these things, I am sure, have influenced this book and its hopeful vision of the future.

Reference Notes

CHAPTER I

1. Warren Johnson and John Hardesty, eds., *Economic Growth vs. the Environment* (Belmont: Wadsworth, 1974), p. 3.
2. Kenneth E. Boulding, "Economics and Ecology," in *Future Environments of North America*, F.F. Darling and J.P. Milton, eds. (Garden City: Natural History Press, 1966), pp. 225-234.
3. Joseph W. Meeker, *The Comedy of Survival: Studies in Literary Ecology* (New York: Scribners, 1974).

CHAPTER II

1. Lionel Tiger and Robin Fox, *The Imperial Animal* (New York: Holt, Rinehart and Winston, 1971); Marshall Sahlins, *Stone Age Economics* (New York: Aldine Publishing Co., 1972); Robert Ardrey, *African Genesis* and *The Hunting Hypothesis* (New York: Atheneum, 1961; 1976); Paul Shepard, *The Tender Carnivore and the Sacred Game* (New York: Scribners, 1973).
2. Marshall D. Sahlins, "The Origins of Society," *Scientific American*, September 1960, pp. 76-87.
3. Richard E. Leakey and Roger Lewin, *Origins* (New York: Dutton, 1977).

4. Colin M. Turnbull, *The Forest People* (New York: Simon and Schuster, 1961); Daisy Bates, *The Passing of the Aborigines: A Lifetime Spent Among the Natives of Australia* (New York: Putnam, 1929); Elizabeth M. Thomas, *The Harmless People* (New York: Knopf, 1959); Laurens Van der Post, *The Heart of the Hunter* (London: Hogarth Press, 1961); Theodora Kroeber, *Ishi in Two Worlds: A Biography of the Last Wild Indian in California* (Berkeley: University of California Press, 1961).

5. Paul Mangelsdorf, "Wheat," *Scientific American*, July 1953, p. 50.

6. Ibid., p. 51.

7 William H. McNeill, *The Rise of the West* (New York: Mentor, 1963), pp. 33-34.

8. Robert J. Braidwood, "The Agricultural Revolution," *Scientific American*, September 1970, pp. 130-148.

9. Robert L. Carneiro, "A Theory of the Evolution of the State," *Science*, August 21, 1970, pp. 733-738.

10. F. H. King, *Farmers of Forty Centuries* (New York: Harcourt, Brace and Co., 1911).

11. U.S. Bureau of the Census, *Historical Statistics of the United States: Colonial Time to 1970* (Washington, D.C.: Government Printing Office), p. 14.

12. Richard Tawney, *Religion and the Rise of Capitalism* (New York: Harcourt, Brace and Co., 1937).

CHAPTER III

1. Richard G. Wilkinson, *Poverty and Progress: An Ecological Perspective on Economic Development* (New York: Praeger, 1973), p. 118.

2. Ibid., p. 123.

3. Karl Polanyi, *The Great Transformation* (Boston: Beacon Press, 1944).

4. David M. Potter, *People of Plenty: Economic Abundance and*

the American Character (Chicago: University of Chicago Press, 1954).

5. National Academy of Sciences, *Mineral Resources and the Environment* (Washington, D.C.: National Academy of Sciences, 1976), pp. 129-130.

6. Stephen E. Kesler, *Our Finite Mineral Resources* (New York: McGraw-Hill, 1976), p. 79.

7. Erick Eckholm and Frank Record, "The Affluent Diet: A Worldwide Health Hazard," *The Futurist*, February 1977, p. 18.

8. Grace Halsell, "Ecuador's Garden of Eden," *The Futurist*, February 1977, p. 18.

9. Earl Cook, *Man, Energy and Society* (San Francisco: W. H. Freeman and Co., 1976), p. 401.

10. M. K. Hubbert, *U.S. Energy Resources: A Review as of 1972*, U.S. Senate Committee on Interior and Insular Affairs, Committee Print Serial 93-40, (Washington, D.C.: Government Printing Office).

11. M. K. Hubbert, "Energy Resources," in *Resources and Man*, Preston Cloud, ed. (San Francisco: W. H. Freeman and Co., 1969), pp. 201-205.

12. Allen L. Hammond, "Coal Research II: Gasification Faces an Uncertain Future," *Science*, August 27 1976, pp. 750-753; and "Coal Research III: Liquefaction Has Far to Go," *Science*, September 3, 1976, pp. 873-875; Thomas Maugh, "Underground Gasification: An Alternative Way to Exploit Coal," *Science*, December 16, 1977, pp. 1132-1134.

13. M. A. Lieberman, "U.S. Uranium Resources: An Analysis of Historical Data," *Science*, April 30, 1976, pp. 431-437.

14. Allen L. Hammond, "Fusion Research," *Science*, July 2, 1976, p. 76.

15. Thomas H. Maugh, "Oil Shale: Prospects on the Upswing. . Again," *Science*, December 9, 1977, pp. 1023-1027.

16. C. C. Burwell, "Solar Biomass Energy: An Overview of U.S Potential," *Science*, March 10, 1978, pp. 1041-1048.

CHAPTER IV

1. "The Use of Energy Around the World," *Resources*, January-March 1977, p. 9.
2. "Researcher Warns of Too Many Machines," *Christian Science Monitor*, January 4, 1978, p. 2.
3. Keith M. Carlson, "Estimates of High-Employment Budgets Changes in Potential Output," *Federal Reserve Bank of St. Louis Review*, August 1977, pp. 16-22.
4. B. R. Hanson, "Energy, Growth, Altruism," Mitchel Prize Paper, Limits to Growth 1975 Conference (Houston, 1975).
5. Henry C. Wallich, "Is There a Capital Shortage?" *Challenge*, September-October 1975, pp. 56-62; Elmore C. Patterson, "Capital Scarcity: How Real Is the Threat?" *Morgan Guaranty Survey*, December 1976, pp. 7-10.
6. "Environment: The Price of Purity," *First Chicago World Report*, September 1976, pp. 1-3.
7. *A Time to Choose: America's Energy Future* (New York: Ford Foundation Energy Policy Project, 1974).
8. E. F. Schumacher, *Small Is Beautiful* (New York: Harper & Row, 1973).
9. Philip Slater, *The Pursuit of Loneliness* (Boston: Beacon Press, 1970).
10. Garrett Hardin, "The Tragedy of the Commons," *Science*, December 13, 1968, pp. 1243-1248.

CHAPTER V

1. Charles E. Lindbloom, "The Science of 'Muddling Through,'" *Public Administration Review*, Spring 1959, pp. 79-88.
2. Walter Lippman, *The Public Philosophy* (New York: Mentor Books, 1956), p. 40.

CHAPTER VI

1. Robert Heilbroner, *An Inquiry into the Human Prospect* (New York: W. W. Norton & Co., 1974).

CHAPTER VII

1. Jane Jacobs, *The Death and Life of Great American Cities* (New York: Vintage Books, 1961).
2. Warren Johnson, "The Case Against Mid-Century Spread," *The Sierra Club Bulletin*, June 1974, p. 14.
3. Scott Burns, *Home, Inc.: The Hidden Wealth and Power of the American Household* (New York: Doubleday, 1975).
4. The most accessible description of The Farm is in *The Mother Earth News*, May-June 1977, pp. 8-20.
5. Warren Johnson, "The Guaranteed Income as an Environmental Measure," in *Toward the Steady State Economy* (San Francisco: W. H. Freeman and Co., 1973).
6. "Voluntary Simplicity," *CoEvolution Quarterly*, Summer 1977, pp. 4-34.

CHAPTER VIII

1. Ruth Benedict, *Patterns of Culture* (Boston: Houghton Mifflin, 1959), pp. 21-22.
2. Lester Brown, *World Population Trends: Signs of Hope, Signs of Stress* (Washington, D. C.: Population Reference Bureau, 1977).
3. See Richard G. Wilkinson, *Poverty and Progress: An Ecological Approach to Development* (New York: Praeger, 1973), ch. 3; Peter Kropotkin, *Mutual Aid* (Boston: Extending Horizons Books, 1902), ch. 3.
4. Peter Freuchen, *Book of the Eskimos* (Greenwich: Fawcett, 1961), pp. 145-154.
5. Robinson Jeffers, "The Bloody Sire," *Selected Poems* (New York: Vintage, 1963).
6. F. G. Bailey, "The Peasant View of the Bad Life," *British Association for the Advancement of Science*, December 1966, pp. 400-401.
7. Kusum Nair, *Blossoms in the Dust* (New York: Praeger, 1961).

CHAPTER IX

1. Robert L. Heilbroner, *The Future as History* (New York: Mentor Books, 1959) p. 199.
2. W. B. Yeats, "The Second Coming," *The Collected Poems of William Butler Yeats* (New York: Macmillan Co., 1951).

Index

adaptation, 14,125,159; as muddling, 23-27; defined, 187-188; inevitability of, 19-23; to environment, 217

abundance, expectation of, 68; pleasures of, 61-63, 182; problems of, 64-68

affluence, difficulty of maintaining, 9, 157-159; diseases of, 91

agriculture, in the future, 100, 181-182; origins of, 39-44; yields, 75-76

animal proteins, 77-78

antibiotics, 96

alternatives, community, 193-196; economic, 189-192

alloying elements, 73

aluminum, 71-72

Amish, 191

atomic energy, *see* nuclear energy

auto industry, 109, 125, 159, 177, 183

Bailey, F. A., 221

balance of payments, 105, 107

barriers, 229; benefits of, 14-19

Benedict, Ruth, 210

Boulding, Kenneth, 15, 43

breeder reactors, 85-86

Briarpatch network, 191

buses, 94

capital, 103, 111, 112-113; costs of, 25

capitalism, 52

change, dangerous rate of, 22, 176-187; fear of, 20; pace of, 27, 171-202; resistance to, 23-24, 31

China, 48, 50

city planning, 150-151

coal, 56-57, 82-84, 90, 94, 110; gasification and liquefaction, 81; resources available, 82-83

coke, 57

collapse, 11, 13, 236

comic hero, 22-23, 168

commune movement, 134, 193-196

community, 13; alternative, 193-196

compromise, 23, 144-145

conservation, of energy, 25;
    through higher prices,
    119-120; versus development,
    172-176
conservationists, *see*
    environmentalists
consumption, of energy, 80;
    falling, 108; and income,
    119,121
cooperation 34-35
copper, 70
corporations, future of,
    111-113
cost of living, 105, 121-122,
    201; in urban areas, 114
crash programs, 125
cultural ecology, 29-30
cultural evolution, 32, 47-48;
    time required, 53-54
cultural imperialism, 227
culture, importance of, 210-211
decentralization, 13, 112, 130,
    218; politics of, 196-200
decentralized industry, 160
democracy, 147, 151
Depression, the Great, 24, 120,
    123, 154, 155, 176, 178
development, versus
    conservation, 172-176
diet, 77-78
disequilibrium, 17-18, 49, 227
dollar, fall in value, 105, 107
due process, 144
Earth Day, 122
ecology, and economics, 14-15;
    and history, 29-30
economic development,
    203-206
economic growth, 154, 157-158

education, 204, 219-220,
    222-223
Emerson, Ralph Waldo, 151
employment, 122-128
energy, 78-90; confusion about,
    79; consumption, 173-174;
    importance of, 69-70; in
    agriculture, 74-78; in
    minerals, 70-74
energy farms, 89
environmental resistance,
    18-19, 122
environmentalists, 79, 146,
    147-148, 180-181
equilibrium, 27; difficulty of
    breaking out of, 16-17
equity, 141
evolution, analogy with
    muddling, 20
experience, as teacher, 21
farm poverty, 64-65
Farm, The, 194-195
federal deficits, 103, 123
federal government, possible
    decline, 165-166
fertilizers, chemical, 74
firewood, 56, 76, 80, 89, 99
fossil fuels, 19, 76, 79, 88
food, 78
forest resources, 60-61
free market, *see* market
    economy
frugality, 9, 14, 21, 162,
    231-232; defined, 12; in
    urban areas, 181-187; with a
    vengeance, 176-181
fusion energy, 86-87
garbage recycling, 95
Garden of Eden, 43-44

Gaskin, Stephen, 194-195
general equilibrium, 16-18
geothermal energy, 88
government, controls, 117,
    133-134, 232; employees,
    162-163; inefficiency, 23-24,
    151; planning, 156-157
group process, 145-147
guaranteed income, 198
Hamilton, Alexander, 133
Hardin, Garrett, 135
health care, and population
    growth, 206-207
Heilbroner, Robert, 153, 233
Henderson, Hazel, 130
heroism, 23
Hobbes, Thomas 33
Homestead Act, 62, 63, 64
homes, fall in value, 177;
    restoration of, 109
horses, 58, 76
household economy, 192, 193
Hubbert, M. K., 80
hunters and gatherers, 32-38
hydroelectric energy, 89
incomes, falling, 108, 116-122,
    162, 201; low, 191; rising,
    102-103
imported resources, 71
India, 48, 50
Indians, American, 210
individual freedom, 134-135
individual responsibilities, 168,
    234
individualism, 44, 234
Industrial Revolution, 53, 55,
    56, 57, 233
industrial society, 11, 12,
    53-54, 69, 100, 233

inequalities, 164; need for,
    164-165
inflation, 9, 11, 50, 121-122,
    126, 127
infrastructure, 206
irrigation, 74
insecticides, 75, 96
Jacobs, Jane, 184
Jeffers, Robinson, 215
Jefferson, Thomas, 117, 128,
    132-135, 169
jobs, 71, 105, 106, 107,
    122-128, 148, 176-178, 183
Johnson, Warren, 14
Keynes, John Maynard, 123
labor, 161, 234; cost of,
    108-111, 121, 123; intensive
    use of, 110; to replace
    machines, 108-109, 123, 128
land, 76, 171, 237; as renew-
    able resource, 99-100; value
    of, 64, 69
Leakey, Richard, 35
limits, see barriers
Lindbloom, Charles, 137-140
Lippman, Walter, 140-143
Luther, Martin, 30
manufacturing, large-scale, 12,
    111-113, 159-162
manufacturing, small-scale, see
    decentralized industry
maladaptation, 188
market, the, 52
market economy, 117, 128-131
    233; early development of,
    58; and technology, 91
Marx, Karl, 30
Marx, Leo, 133
Meeker, Joseph, 22-23

methane, 98
mobility, 233-234
modern values, 13
muddling, analogy with evolu-
    tion, 20-21; benefits of,
    149-151; as political adapta-
    tion, 23-27; and unemploy-
    ment, 124-125
muddling through, 137-169;
    hazards of, 153-169
Nair, Kusum, 222
national parks, 61, 63, 141, 148
natural gas, 66-68, 75, 79-80;
    price controls on, 105,
    117-118
natural resources, 15, 54,
    55-100; abundance of, 64;
    restraints provided by, 19;
    role of technology, 69-74; in
    underdeveloped countries,
    204-205; see renewable and
    nonrenewable resources.
niche, of industrial society, 18,
    96, 187; consumption of, 19,
    96; discovery of, 56, 135
nonrenewable resources, 19,
    32, 68
nuclear energy, 80, 84-88;
    breeder reactors, 85-86, 88;
    fusion reactors, 86-88
oblivion, 11
ocean technology, 88
oil, 59, 66-68, 79-80; imports,
    105-107; 87-88; price
    controls, 105, 117-118;
oil shales, 88
Organization of Petroleum
    Exporting Countries, OPEC,
    102

overpopulation, 203, 205, 215,
    227
overshoot and collapse, 24, 180
petroleum, see oil
planning, 26, 156-158
Plato, 151
political adaptation, 23-27
politicians, difficulties of,
    25-26, 139, 141-142, 146-147
Polanyi, Karl, 59
pollution, 115; taxes, 21
population growth, 18, 74,
    207-209; end of, 211-216;
    control of, 37-38, 39,
    212-216, 228
potlatch, 37
predators, 17-18
predestination, and capitalism,
    51-52
prices, and conservation,
    119-120; and cost of pro-
    duction, 67-78; and environ-
    mental resistance, 122;
    falling, 64-65; of food, 66; of
    land, 100; and the market,
    130, 190; of oil and gas,
    84, 105-106; of raw materi-
    als, 101-111; rising, 11, 25,
    68, 232; and technological
    feasibility, 90-91
price controls, 25, 105-106,
    172
primogeniture, 61
profits, windfall, 106
Protestantism, 50
public interest, the, 139-149
railroads, 114
rapid transit, 93-94
rationality, in politics, 141

raw material prices, 101-111; relative to labor, 108-113
Reformation, the, 47, 51
regional differences, 115-116
religion, in early civilization, 46-48
Renaissance, 13, 18, 50
renewable resources, 21, 68, 97-100, 171, 182, 217; safety of, 22
resiliency, of life, 16
responsibility, 13, 167-169
risk, of alternatives, 191-192, 198
Rockefeller, John D., 67
rural areas, depopulation, 66; preference for 185-186
Sahlins, Marshall, 34
scapegoats, 19
scale, or energy use, 80-81
scarcity, 12, 14, 25, 31, 84, 102, 120, 121, 156, 197; adjustments to, 116, 130; changes in, 72-73; efforts to deny, 22, 121, 125
Schumacher, E. F., 128
science and technology, 18, 44
scientific knowledge, 237
selflessness, 35
self-centeredness, 234
service industries, 115
sex, control of, 34
skills, 183
Smith, Adam, 128, 132-135
soil erosion, 65
solar energy, 88, 97-98
space travel, 92-93
space program, 156
special interests, 145-147

stability, 9, 16
stagflation, 121, 124, 127
state and local government, 166
steel, 72
supersonic transport, SST, 91-92
survival, 11, 23
tax, credits, 128; on energy, 140; rebated, 119-120; revenues, 162, 178
technological advance, 55-60, 68, 229; problems of, 64
technology, failing, 90-96; industrial, 89-90, 95, 108-109, 233; simple, 97-100; in underdeveloped countries, 209-210
time, 22, 237; for cultural evolution, 53-54; for new energy sources, 81; importance of, 171-172, 175
trade, hazards of, 224-226
traditional societies, 16, 58-59, 205, 216
traditional virtues, 13, 129, 234-235
tragic hero, 22-23
transportation, 12-13, 58, 63, 74, 91, 114, 123, 160; air, 109; energy use in, 110-111; high-speed, ground, 93-94
underdeveloped countries, advantages of, 216-219; prospects of, 203-228
unemployment, 11, 105, 122-123, 162, 177-178, 232; rural, 201
unions, labor, 161
U. S. Forest Service, 61

uranium, 85
urban areas, future of,
    113-116; high density, 184;
    and renewable resources, 99
urban renewal, 21, 94-95, 140
utopia, 11
Vietnam War, 26, 154-155, 157
violence, 22, 231-232

voluntary simplicity, 201
welfare, 119, 177-178
White, E. B., 151
Western civilization, 13, 49-53
will, loss of, 13
wind power, 98
women, and agriculture, 39-41
Yeats, William B., 235